NORMANDY

Arthur Eperon is o[...] st-known
travel writers in Eu[...] 5 he has
worked as a journali[...] ng travel.
He has concentrate[...] enty-five
years and contribute[...] *he Times*,
the *Daily Telegraph*, [...] *Popular Motoring* and *TV Times*. He has also appeared on radio and television and for five years was closely involved in Thames Television's programme *Wish You Were Here*. He has been wine writer to the RAC publications and a number of magazines.

He has an intimate and extensive knowledge of France and its food and wine as a result of innumerable visits there over the last forty years. In 1974 he won the Prix des Provinces de France, the annual French award for travel writing.

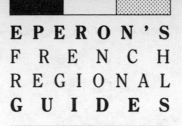

NORMANDY

ARTHUR EPERON

PAN BOOKS
LONDON, SYDNEY AND AUCKLAND

First published 1990 by Pan Books Ltd
Cavaye Place, London SW10 9PG
9 8 7 6 5 4 3 2 1
© Arthur Eperon 1989
Illustrations © Mary Fraser 1989
Maps © Ken Smith 1989

ISBN 0 330 312073

Designed by Peter Ward
Photoset by Parker Typesetting Service Leicester
Printed and bound in Great Britain by
Richard Clay Ltd, Bungay, Suffolk

CONTENTS

1 *Departments of France*

KEY TO PRICES

MEALS   A = Under 75F   ROOMS   A = Under 100F
         B = 75–90F   B = 100–150F
         C = 90–125F   C = 150–200F
         D = 125–150F   D = 200–250F
         E = 150–175F   E = 250–350F
         F = 175–225F   F = 350–450F
         G = over 225F   G = over 450F

Room prices per night for double room without breakfast.
Meals include tax and service.

INTRODUCTION

Normandy is a rich, lush land farmed by a people apart. Normans never do anything by halves. They work hard, eat heartily and drink deep. That is the essence of Normandy and its people. The thought of a Norman farmer sitting down to a 'modern' meal with a couple of slices of half-raw duck and slivers of carrot and kiwi fruit for decoration is unimaginable. He would want the whole duck in a rich cream sauce with mountains of steaming potatoes and carrots. Not so long ago Norman farmers put bowls of thick cream on their tables to ladle into their soup. Cream, butter, cider and the apple spirit called calvados are still used lavishly in Norman kitchens and there is no evidence that Normans die earlier than any other Frenchmen. The true *trou Normand*, the stomach settler taken in the middle of a meal, is not the modern version of apple sorbet with a thimbleful of calvados poured over it, but a good slug of calvados swallowed neat and quickly.

I met a Norman farmer once by accident in a local hotel and he invited me to a 'small meal' with his family. It was a formidable feast, with sauces thick with cream, cider and mushrooms and lovely fresh vegetables. Our *trou* was an Englishman's treble of calvados made on the farm. After the meal I was given café Calva, coffee with another good measure of calvados, followed by a *rincette* of calvados to rinse the mouth. Then came a *gloria* – yet another calvados, repeated twice. I was returned to my little *logis* in a horse-drawn cart – which was at least safer than driving, if bumpier.

Normans are proud to be rural and want to stay that way. The variety of scenery is captivating. From Dieppe, to which the packet boats from Newhaven were in daily service by the 1850s, the coast westward is of chalk cliffs and pebble beaches, with villages hidden in the coastal clefts or in folds behind the cliffs. Past the Seine estuary begin the great beaches, once the play-

grounds of Parisians and centres of the smart set until motor-
ways and jets swept them away to further shores. Deauville and
Trouville, Houlgate and Cabourg still have that air of their *belle
époque* heyday, even to their old Grand Hotels. D-Day in 1944
changed the rest of this coast for ever. The new houses, hotels
and shops of the little family resorts still look self-conscious and
not quite sure that they should be there. Since the D-Day anni-
versary in 1984 these villages and beaches have had a boom in
visitors unknown since the 1920s. The east side of the Cotentin
Peninsula, with Cherbourg at the top, starts with wild coastal
stretches, and seas can be very perverse, as the Americans discovered when they were landing in 1944. Northward are some
delightful old fishing villages like St-Vaast-la-Hougue, renowned for oysters, and Barfleur, now the joy of yachtsmen.

The rugged north coast has spectacular spots like the *corniche* road from Barfleur to Cherbourg and the wild granite rock
Cap de la Hague west of Cherbourg. Here at Goury is one of the
most vital lifeboat stations in Europe, which has saved hundreds
of sailors from the frightening Alderney Race. At Nez de
Jobourg just south, a mile walk brings you to a grandiose view of
the racing sea and fatal rocks. From the tip you can see the
British Channel Isles of Alderney, Sark, Guernsey and Jersey,
called *Les Iles Anglo-Normandes* by the Normans. The isles have
been English since William the Conqueror, Duke of Normandy,
took the English crown in 1066.

Down this west coast are a series of old fishing villages.
Some, like Barneville-Carteret, Coutainville, Granville and St-

Jean-le-Thomas, were little family resorts by the turn of the century and still have their faithful devotees. The view from St-Jean-le-Thomas across the sandbanks and quicksands to the old abbey of Mont-St-Michel so impressed Allied Commander-in-Chief General Eisenhower that he mentioned it in his war memoirs.

In north Cotentin Peninsula the land is less fertile than much of Normandy. It is littered with rock. Here is the true *bocage* – little fields criss-crossed with hedges, trees, and little lanes hiding behind banks which in spring are covered first with millions of yellow primroses, then foxgloves. No one would dream of calling these wild flowers weeds and applying chemical killers. As you go south the grass is lusher and there are many more cows feeding on it. These days not all are the traditional Norman brown-and-white with rings round their eyes. But they produce the same rich milk and cream. This is still *bocage* country and you can see easily enough how this area of Normandy's countryside changed the Allied invasion plans on the Cherbourg Peninsula. Highly mechanised American units which had landed at Utah Beach simply could not get along the narrow lanes or over the banks. The US army had to take to its feet, like the Paratroopers and the British Commandos. Overnight, they had to learn a new way of fighting. Hedges were such a handicap that where they could use tanks, they fitted bulldozer blades to them and had to take the terrain literally hedge by hedge.

The south-west side of the peninsula becomes flat and the whole bay of Mont-St-Michel empties in spring and autumn low

tides, when the sea retreats for nine miles, leaving lush pastures where sheep graze to produce the great *pré-salé* (salt meadow) lambs with a subtle, distinctive flavour. Beware of quicksands in the bay. The old monks knew their way across but their enemies did not.

The villages and towns behind the landing beaches of Calvados have been rebuilt, especially Caen, but the countryside is serene again and delightful. Avoid the main roads and explore.

When I was young and very fit I wandered on foot through the rich countryside of Calvados below Bayeux, along the wooded Orne valley, where beech and oak still outnumber predatory, sombre pines, and into the hills, forests and rocks of the grandly-named Suisse-Normande. I would willingly have lived there. Now that I must mostly motor, I can still reach many of my old secret haunts by taking delightful lanes still nearly deserted. I can still enjoy the May-time apple blossom of the Auge valley, outshining even my corner of the Kent Weald, and the wild yellow irises in the ditches.

Until very recently this was a truly secretive land, little known to any foreigners except keen walkers and climbers. It was hardly known to the French at all.

The new and deservedly successful Brittany Ferries route Portsmouth–Caen (which really goes to Ouistreham) has brought a few more explorers to this delicious part of Normandy but most who cross by ferry are hurrying to their gîtes further south or to beaches. Too many turn straight onto the A13 motorway from Caen to Rouen and Paris. The Calvados stretch of this motorway is one of the dreariest in Europe. The Suisse-Normande, a delightful blend of rocks, gorges and escarpments, with the river Orne fighting its way through, and of gentle hills and green secret valleys, is one of the gems of France's varied countryside.

Britons tend to call the whole area 'Calvados', from Bayeux and Caen and the rich Pays d'Auge south of Deauville (which *are* in Calvados) to the Suisse-Normande, which is mostly in l'Orne and the fine forests of Normandie Maine. The Eure area, which stretches eastward from Calvados and Orne to the Seine and over the river above Rouen, is heavily and attractively wooded. Walking in its woods and forests is a great pleasure.

The forest of Lyons, with superb old and enormous beeches and oaks, is the loveliest. Further south and east between the valleys of the Seine and Eure rivers, many Parisians have bought houses in small, sleepy villages as weekend retreats. In a huge bend of the Seine between Rouen and Le Havre, by the convenient and spectacular Brotonne bridge, is Brotonne forest, designated a *Parc Naturel Régional* in 1974 and now a haven of peace for walking and picnics. Though the D913 road from the bridge inevitably carries a fair amount of traffic, the smaller D131 turning off it is a lovely road, and so is the even less important local D40 – a little stretch of France which is a joy to anyone who loves peaceful woodlands.

The Seine valley has been much industrialised and in many places no longer seems to belong to Normandy – not even the new part of Rouen south of the river. But some delightful stretches and charming old villages have survived, such as the riverside village of La Bouille downriver from Rouen, which the painter Monet loved, and the Forest of Roumare across the river-bank. The north bank from Amfreville upstream to historic Les Andelys and on to Vernon is charming, too, with views of many little islands.

The Pays de Caux, north of the Seine to Dieppe, is of rolling chalk hills with prosperous farms and half-timbered farmhouses like the Tudor farms and cottages of the Kent Weald. Some stretches of country grow sugar beet and are monotonous, but the valleys of the little rivers such as the Durdent and Saane are charming.

Dieppe is France's oldest seaside resort and has two pleasant forests within easy driving distance – Eawy (pronounced locally e-a-vi), 6475 hectares with superb beeches and the Forest of Eu, with marked paths for walking through, lovely groves of beech and oak. It is on the northern border of Normandy marked by the river Bresle.

Eawy is in the Pays de Bray, a truly rich countryside of woods and meadows, the 'dairy of Paris', where cheese-making is an industry. It is rich in orchards, too, producing dessert apples and cider.

Thirty years ago I described Dieppe as 'instant France' – a port where you only had to step off the ferry to be a francophile.

Dieppe Harbour

Perhaps I should have called it 'instant Normandy', for the fruits of the earth and sea have been good to the Normans through centuries, they have suffered less poverty than almost any part of France and they have an almost smug independence of Paris, its political manoeuvrings, its fashions and its enthusiasms.

HOW TO GO

BOAT FROM BRITAIN
Newhaven–Dieppe (Sealink-Dieppe Ferries: 4 hrs).
Portsmouth–Le Havre (P & O: 5½ hrs).

Portsmouth–Caen (Ouistreham) (Brittany Ferries: 6 hrs).
Portsmouth–Cherbourg (Sealink; P & O: 4¾ hrs).
Weymouth–Cherbourg (Sealink: 4 hrs).
Poole–Cherbourg (Brittany Ferries, end May–mid September: 4½ hrs day, 6 hrs night).
Portsmouth–St-Malo (just over Brittany border) (Brittany Ferries: 9 hrs).
Short Channel crossings Dover/Folkestone–Calais/Boulogne (Sealink; P & O; Hoverspeed hovercraft) and Ramsgate–Dunkirk (Sally Line) all land within 180–250 km of Dieppe and Rouen.

AIR
Gatwick–Rouen (Air Vendée), Gatwick–Le Havre (Brit Air), Gatwick–Caen (Brit Air), Gatwick–Deauville (Summer: Lucas/ Aigle Azur) – all booked in Britain through Air France, 158 New Bond Street, London W1Y 0AY (tel. 071-499-9511). Contact them for air connections between Normandy and other French cities, including Paris.

RAIL
Good rail network from Paris direct or indirect to many Norman towns. Central and most coastal towns served from Paris St-Lazare station; southern towns from Montparnasse station. St-Lazare to Le Havre, Dieppe or Caen takes about 2 hrs, to Cherbourg 4 hrs.

FOOD

The fanatical enthusiasm for *nouvelle cuisine* has died down. Chefs are flirting with new phrases like 'modern regional', 'new classical' and 'light traditional' cuisine. The young French are hurrying through hamburgers from Macdonalds, and gourmets in and outside France have begun to ask plaintively 'Whatever happened to *French* cuisine?'

I am tempted to tell them that French cuisine is alive and well and living in Normandy. Certainly, great regional dishes remain mostly uncorrupted in Normandy itself, even if chefs outside the area may cut corners in their *sole normande* or *à la dieppoise* and their apple tarts.

See a cow chewing the succulent grass of an orchard and you have the basis of Norman cooking – butter, cream, creamy cheese, apples, cider and calvados. Tripe, too, of course. Add the lambs from the salt marshes of southern Cotentin, fresh fish landed by the fleets of Fécamp, Dieppe and small ports of the Cotentin, and Rouen duck which now comes from Yvetot, and the menu is nearly complete. But pigs are important, too – fed often on windfall apples and pears and skimmed milk.

Normandy butter is considered to be the best in France and most chefs consider butter from the area of the little port of Isigny, west of Bayeux, the best in Normandy.

Local markets are delightful. Here you can still buy real farm produce and freshly landed fish. Dieppe's Saturday market, spilling out from Grand'Rue into side roads, is a revelation in days of EEC conformity, with butter still sold from great slabs made in local dairies, oysters often at very low price, real farm free-range chickens and lovely farm-made cheeses.

There are good fish markets at Fécamp, charming Honfleur, Cherbourg and inland at Rouen and Caen. The most popular fish are sole, turbot and *barbue* (brill, a lesser turbot, which the French like). Dieppe is known for mackerel (*maquereau* – sometimes called *lisettes*). Mussels, clams (*praires*) and oysters are favourite shellfish. Oyster centres include Courseulles-sur-Mer, Dives, Luc and St-Vaast-la-Hougue.

Coquilles Saint-Jacques (scallops) and *crevettes* (*grises* are shrimps, *roses* are prawns) are eaten a lot, as are *bigorneaux* (winkles) in mixed shellfish platters. *Demoiselles de Cherbourg* are delicious young lobsters. Dieppe scallops are world famous.

Sole is the star of Normandy fish. In the true old *sole normande* the fish is poached in cider and cream and the sauce thickened with cream and eggs. Many chefs have their own versions (adding mushrooms, perhaps, with prawns or mussels) and outside Normandy most chefs cook the sole in wine then add cream to make the sauce, which is not authentically *à la normande*. Cider in cooking gives a more delicate flavour than wine.

Sole à la dieppoise is delicious. Originally the fish was cooked in very dry cider and shallots but now even Normans sometimes use wine. Cream and butter is added to the juices and this is reduced to a smooth, velvety sauce. Mussels should be creamed into the sauce, too, but often mussels are simply poached in wine with prawns and used as garnish.

Sauce normande these days can be almost any thick sauce with real cream and cider, calvados or both. For fish it is usually based on a *fumet* (fish stock) and cream. *Marmite* (or *matelote*) *dieppoise* is a mixed sea-fish stew, ideally with sole, turbot, monkfish (*lotte*), scallops and other shellfish cooked in cider with *cerfeuil* (chervil), sometimes tomatoes but always cream.

One fish dish *without* cream is sole (or turbot) *au cidre* – cooked whole with chopped shallots and parsley in very dry cider. Dieppe mackerel is also cooked this way.

Fécamp has had salted cod (*morue*) and herrings since the 10th century and has been smoking them since the 13th century, and little Honfleur was selling salted cod to Far Eastern countries in return for spices in the 16th century.

Omelette normande as a starter is usually stuffed with mushrooms and shrimps in a cream sauce. The dessert version is an omelette made with cream, filled with apple softened in calvados and butter.

Charcuterie includes many *pâtés* and *terrines*. Brawn is good. Black pudding (*boudin*) is almost a cult in Perche. At Mortagne-au-Perche, a Brotherhood of Pudding Tasters runs an annual contest for the best black pudding, luring contestants from all over western Europe, including Lancashire, which wins some of the prizes.

Chitterling sausages (*andouille* and *andouillette*) from Vire and Caen are particularly famous (or notorious, according to your taste). They are best when smoked and grilled, and should be washed down with cider. The big Vire version is usually sliced and served as a starter.

Another famous local dish which rouses passions of pleasure or distaste is *tripes à la mode de Caen* – pieces of prepared tripe (cow's stomach) layered with onions, leeks, carrots, cloves and a *bouquet garni* (thyme, parsley, bay) and two split calves feet to make jelly, cooked either in water and calvados or cider with a little calvados for anything from eight to forty-eight hours. Even Normans now buy the dish ready-made in jars.

Rouen ducklings which come from Yvetot and Duclair are a special breed (crossed domestic and wild). It is in Rouen and Paris that *caneton rouennais* is made, stuffed with its own liver, roasted and served with a sauce of its cooking juices, cream and blood squeezed from the carcass by a special press. It's a controversial dish, for the ducklings are strangled or suffocated to keep in the blood, which gives it a gamy flavour. More tolerable to most modern gourmets is duck or chicken *Vallée d'Auge*. Many chefs have their own recipes for this delightful dish, but all include plenty of cream, and flambéing the chicken in calvados.

The same cooking method and sauce are used for trout, for game birds and for veal.

Game is plentiful in the Suisse-Normande, especially pheasant, partridge, woodcock and trout. Game birds are often cooked *à la normande*. They are turned in butter until golden, put in a casserole and packed around with slices of cooking and dessert apples turned in butter. After cooking in a moderate oven for an hour, cream and calvados are stirred into the apple mixture and the whole cooked for another five minutes uncovered. Duck is excellent cooked this way.

Traditionally Normans cook meat in *graisse normande* (clarified pork fat and suet, flavoured with vegetables and herbs), which you can buy in cardboard pots in some butchers' and *charcuteries*. A delightful dish is *épaule à la crème* – a shoulder of lamb on the bone marinaded overnight in very dry cider, calvados, onions, garlic, pepper and herbs (including rosemary, of course), browned in butter and cooked gently in its fat, flour and the marinade. Egg and cream are whisked into the juices to make the sauce.

The traditional local desserts are still *bourdelos* (apple baked in suet crust – called *douillons* when pears are used) and *tarte normande* (apple tarts made in dozens of ways, sometimes with almonds). The version of apple tart I learned from an old chef in a Dieppe cookery school years ago was a short-pastry flan half-filled with cooking apples stewed in a little cider and sugar, topped with overlapping slices of eating apples soaked in calvados and sprinkled with sugar. Apricot jam is used as a glaze. All apple tarts are served covered with cream, of course.

A delicious dessert from pâtisseries is *mirliton* – a puff-pastry tart filled with almond paste, egg yolks and sugar. Chocolates flavoured with calvados are delicious too. Fillings are flavoured, too, with Bénédictine from Fécamp.

CHEESES

Even by French standards, Normandy is rich in cheeses, with more than thirty fairly well-known varieties and many still made on farms. Seek them in local markets. Most are soft, white-coated, though washed-rind cheeses are found in Pays de Bray. Camembert was certainly mentioned by Thomas Corneille, brother of playwright Pierre, in his dictionary in 1708. But Marie Harel, a farmer's wife from Camembert village, takes the credit for it and has her statue in the modern square of nearby Vimoutiers, donated by a US cheese company. It seems that she improved it and marketed it in 1790 with the help of a priest she was hiding during the French Revolution. It became fashionable last century when it was presented to Napoleon III as he opened the Paris–Granville railway. Then in 1890 a Paris company invented the little round wooden boxes and sent the cheese round the world. Now factory versions, *pasteurisé*, are produced in sixty-seven *départements* of France but the real thing comes from the Norman *départements* of Calvados, Eure, Manche, Orne and Seine-Maritime. It is made from cows' milk and cured for three weeks. Real farm-made cheeses are hard to find but can be tracked down at country markets. Gourmets claim that camembert should be firm and even chalky but some of the best I have eaten have almost met me at the farmhouse door.

Livarot, another truly great cheese of Normandy, is older than Camembert. I love its strong, pungent smell and delicate spicy flavour, though my wife Barbara has been known to mention drains. Made only in Pays d'Auge and quite scarce, it is

matured in a cave for at least a month. The rind is a shiny reddish-brown colour. Small cheeses are called Petits Lisieux.

Pont-l'Évêque, an old farm cheese, dates from the Middle Ages, when it was called *angelot*. It is rectangular, matured for one or two months in a humid cave, and is marketed in a wooden box. Its rind is almost orange, its taste sweet, and it should be soft but not runny. Its criss-cross crust comes from being dried on straw mats.

Other Norman cheeses well worth seeking include:
Bricquebec – soft, yellow, robust, from Bricquebec abbey.
Brillat-Savarin – delightful, mild cheese, but not for slimmers (75% fat, triple cream). Invented by Henri Androuet in the 1930s, named after the great gastronome, the real thing made only in Rouvray-Catillon, near Forges-les-Eaux in Pays de Bray.
Carré de Bray – small, square, salty, slightly tart; farmers' version of Neufchâtel.
Coeur de Bray – soft, supple, fruity.
Demi-sel – uncured, moist, small, low-salt, mild; invented last century in Gournay-en-Bray. Foil-wrapped.
Excelsior – little brother of Brillat-Savarin and nearly as fatty and creamy. Fin-de-Siècle is similar.
Fromage de Monsieur – firm, smelly, fruity cheese from Roumois plateau between Auge and Caux was invented by a farmer actually called Monsieur Fromage!
Lucullus – nutty, triple-cream, 75% fat factory cheese from Évreux and also Brie in Ile-de-France.
Mignot – fruity farm cheese from Pays d'Auge produced autumn and winter, eaten with sweet cider.
Neufchâtel – dates back to 10th century. Moussey, delicate, lasting flavour; eaten fresh (*fleuri*) with fruit or strong and ripe (*affiné*).
Pavé d'Auge (also called Pavé de Moyaux) – superb spicy, strong cheese made for centuries.
Petit-Suisse – soft, fresh, unsalted cheese, often sugared and eaten with fruit. Now made all over France but invented by a Bray farm wife and her Swiss cowherd in 1850.
Trouville – farm-made Pont-l'Évêque.

When buying cheese remember the French phrases for three ripenesses of cheese. '*Pas trop fait*' means under-ripe or fresh, '*à point*' means just right, '*bien fait*' means so ripe that it could run around the plate.

In the cheese town of Livarot, between Lisieux and Vimoutiers, at 16 rue l'Évêque, is the modest-looking, grandly-named Conservatoire des Techniques Fromagères where they make good camembert, Pont-l'Évêque and Livarot. The creamy Livarot, wrapped traditionally in sedge-reeds from the river Vie, uses five litres of milk to make 250 grams of cheese, compared with two litres for the camembert. Conducted tours with an explanation of cheese-making methods and tastings costs fifteen francs.

DRINK

No wine is made now in Normandy. The slopes are too fertile for wine grapes. But cider is made here very similarly to wine. The best comes from Pays d'Auge, is still or very slightly *pétillant* (sparkling) and carries the 'Cidre de la Vallée d'Auge' label. It can be sweet or so dry that it seems to disappear on your palate before it hits your throat. Best centres are Pont-l'Évêque, Livarot, Bonnebosc, Vimoutiers and Cambremer. 'Le Duc' cider is made traditionally at Anneville-sur-Cie, near Longueville, Pays de Caux. You can visit the *cidrerie* called Duché de Longueville.

Most popular with tourists, especially Parisians, is the fizzy *cidre bouché* which comes in bottles with a wired cork since fermentation continues in the bottle. It's all right as an aperitif but not for drinking with rich creamy Norman dishes. *Poiré* is pear-cider (perry) – still or fizzy.

A fashionable new drink from Livarot is 'Deauville', a fizzy 'cider' of apples and peaches. More likely to last is the aperitif Pommeau, made like the old ratafias of Burgundy and Champagne – in this case with five parts unfermented apple juice (instead of grape juice) and one part calvados (instead of marc), served iced. You can make a tolerable version at home.

Calvados, Normandy's apple spirit, can either be wonderful or it can be like battery acid. Farmers still make it illegally and some sell it. Some 'calvados fermier' is good and worth following the roadside signs for. The worst, not true calvados, is officially called *eau-de-vie de cidre*. Pack a jar with peaches and a little sugar, top it up with this liquor, screw it down and leave for at least a month – preferably six months. You have a splendid dessert and quaffable drink. Next grade is 'Calvados Appellation Réglementée', distilled from cider from specific areas. The best calvados is Pays d'Auge. It must be made from Pays d'Auge cider and double-distilled in pot stills. It is aged in casks and improves greatly, like single-malt whisky, over years. Fine calvados is two or three years old. LVSOP is at least five years old, with at least four in barrel. Napoléon, Hors d'Age and Age Inconnu are at least six years old, with five in barrel, but often twelve to fifteen years old. It takes thirty litres of cider to produce one litre of calvados. One big distillery where you can see it made and taste it free is Distillerie Boulard at Coquainvilliers, eight km north-west of Lisieux.

Many Normans still take a café calva – black coffee and slug of calvados – for breakfast.

Bénédictine liqueur is produced now in a huge factory at Fécamp which crowds of people visit in summer to taste the nectar (Easter–mid-November 9–11.15 a.m., 2–6 p.m.; winter Monday–Friday only). But it was first produced by a Venetian monk (from Fécamp monastery), Dom Barnado Vincelli, in 1510 because he needed a warming elixir to ward off the chill winter winds of Fécamp. He used twenty-seven herbs and spices, some growing wild on the local cliffs. Production stopped with the French Revolution but was revived in 1863 when a local historian, Alexander Legrand, found three scribbled recipes among old abbey documents – for a *menthe*, a healing balm, and Vincelli's complicated elixir recipe. To produce the liqueur Legrand had a veritable palace built by the architect Albert, follower of Viollet-le-Duc. Part Gothic, part Renaissance, and entirely ostentatious, it also houses a museum of the drink and works of art saved from the monastery. Bénédictine liqueur has been immortalised in works of Gauguin and Rousseau and had bottle labels designed by Cappiello, Lopes Silva, Mucha and Sam.

HISTORY AND ART

Statue of William the Conqueror, Falaise

The history of Normandy began for most Britons with the invasion of England in 1066 by William the Conqueror, known to the rest of France as William the Bastard. It began for most Normans in the 8th century when the Norsemen started to arrive each spring in their longboats to rape, pillage and burn far inland, then disappear in the autumn with loot and prisoners. It must have come as a big surprise in 911 when the Norse Earl Rollo made a peace treaty with the Frankish King

Charles the Simple (meaning honest), was baptised a Christian and settled down as Robert, Duke of Normandy, with his followers to breed cattle and children and keep out the other Norsemen and Danes. The Norsemen even adopted the French language but did not give up the great Viking tradition of producing many children by several wives and concubines.

But back in 52 BC the Gauls of this area were already putting up a last stand against Julius Caesar's Roman armies, and when the Romans took over, the Gallo-Romans (locals supporting the Romans) set up ports at Rouen, Honfleur and Lillebonne to trade with England. The Roman rule was broken around the 4th century AD by invaders from north and east – Alamans, Goths and Franks. Clovis, the Frankish king, took over and as he had become a Christian in 496, Christianity came in, with bishoprics at Bayeux and Rouen, then in other towns such as Sées and Évreux. In the 7th century Bénédictine abbeys were established at Rouen, St-Wandrille, Jumièges and Fécamp. These were duly looted by the Norsemen but were re-established once the Norman settlers became Christians. William the Conqueror in particular encouraged the Bénédictines to re-establish themselves and rebuild the abbeys. His capital was Rouen but he set up a second capital at Caen, with an abbey which he built and a nunnery built by his wife Matilda. This was to placate the Pope who had excommunicated them because they had married, despite the fact that they were cousins. Lanfranc, the monk who was William's friend and adviser, persuaded the Pope to change his mind.

William was the son of Robert the Magnificent, Duke of Normandy, and a Falaise tanner's daughter – a proud girl who disdained being smuggled into the Duke's castle and rode in openly. When he became Duke, William decided to marry his cousin Matilda of Flanders. She said that she would rather become a nun than marry a bastard, so he rode to Lille, seized her by her plaits, dragged her round her room and kicked her. The lady, deciding that such angry ardour deserved rewarding, relented and married him!

Counter threats from France to the Duchy of Normandy made William strengthen ties with England and the future King Edward the Confessor of England took refuge in Rouen. When

Edward went back to claim his throne in 1042, he took with him
Norman advisers and churchmen. In 1050 Edward asked for
Normandy's military help, in return, William said later, for
making William heir to the English throne. When Edward died,
the Saxon Harold was proclaimed King of England. In 1066 the
infuriated William persuaded the King of Norway to invade
England in the north while he landed in the south to claim what
the Bayeux tapestry and Normans called his 'rightful crown'.
Harold defeated the Viking army at Stamford Bridge, then
marched south, where he met the Norman invaders just outside
Hastings. The Normans feigned defeat and retreat to lure the
Saxons from behind their defences, turned and defeated them.
Harold was killed by an arrow through the eye. William, Duke of
Normandy, became King of England, and cruelly subjugated
the Anglo-Saxons, who heartily detested both him and the Normans. He divided England among his followers, making them
earls. Even his cook, William de Percy, said to have fought nobly
at the Battle of Hastings using a huge soup spoon as a cudgel,
was given vast lands from Essex to Yorkshire, made an earl and
his descendants became Dukes of Northumberland.

When William the Conqueror was killed fighting the King of
France, his eldest son Robert became Duke of Normandy, his
second son William Rufus became King William II of England.
They were soon fighting, but the youngest brother Henry, born
in England, took the English throne as Henry I when William
Rufus died, then captured Normandy from his brother Robert
and withstood all attacks by the King of France. So did his
grandson Henry II (Henry Plantagenet) and *his* son Richard
Lionheart. But the weak King John of England, Richard's
brother, lost Normandy to the clever and determined King of
France, Philippe Auguste.

Henry V of England, victor of Agincourt, took Normandy
back in 1415 and Normans still revere his Regent, John, Duke of
Bedford, who among other benefits, founded the University of
Caen and established two of the most beautiful Gothic churches
in Rouen. Henry V married the daughter of the King of France
and was declared heir to the French throne. After his death Joan
of Arc, by her victory at Orléans, roused the frightened Dauphin, hereditary heir, who was in virtual hiding on the Loire, to

action and finally persuaded him to be crowned. But Normandy remained English. After Joan's capture by the Burgundians and brutal burning as a 'heretic' by the English in Rouen, her great companion-in-arms, Jean Dunois (the Bastard of Orléans) gradually drove the English out of France for the Dauphin, now King Charles VII of France, finally forcing them from Normandy in 1450. The Dukedom of Normandy disappeared in 1469, though the Queen of England is still technically 'Duke of Normandy'.

In the Wars of Religion, Normandy was a hotbed of Protestantism, especially in Caen, with its university, and the seaports which had been influenced by contact with England and Holland. When Louis XIV made Protestantism illegal in 1685, there was a mass emigration of Protestants from Normandy. As many were very skilled artisans, Normandy's economy was in tatters for a while and this rich land knew poverty.

Meanwhile the seamen of Honfleur, Le Havre and Dieppe were ranging the New World and opening up regions of North and South America. In the 15th century Jean de Béthencourt discovered the Canary Islands and set himself up as king. Quebec was founded as a Norman colony by Samuel de Champlain of Dieppe. In 1635 Pierre Belain d'Esnambuc took over Martinique, then Guadeloupe – both West Indian isles which are still a part of 'Metropolitan France', with its people voting for representatives in the French Parliament. And in 1682 Robert Cavalier, Sieur de La Salle, from Rouen, descended the Ohio and Mississippi rivers to the sea, taking possession of Louisiana.

The Prussians occupied Upper Normandy briefly during the Franco-Prussian War of 1870–71 but they were kept quiet with a ration of a litre of calvados per man each day and threats of British intervention stopped them occupying the ports.

Even the 1914–18 War left Normandy unscathed by standards of most of northern France, but in the three months of 1944 after the D-Day Allied landings to free Europe, two million men fought in Normandy and the destruction was horrific. Not only villages by landing beaches but dozens of small towns and big cities were nearly obliterated. Le Havre port was completely destroyed. So was Caen and its neighbouring factories. In Le Havre (population 180,000) five thousand civilians were killed, tens of thousands left homeless. The recovery of Normandy has been almost incredible.

Two very important events in Normandy's history were the building of Le Havre port in 1517 because Harfleur was silted-up, and the opening of the railway from Paris to Rouen in 1843. Previously the river journey could be very unpredictable. Rouen was able to build up as a port, so that now it is the fifth biggest in France.

Railways were built with British know-how and British work-men, who had their own English-language newspapers. Railways to the coast launched Normandy's tourist trade. The flighty Duchess of Berry had already started the fashion for sea-bathing in 1824 at Dieppe. Previously sea-water was drunk as a cure for all sorts of ills.

It was seascapes and vivid coastal light which lured many great artists to the Normandy coast. Richard Bonington, the English watercolour painter, painted the still-deserted coast from 1801 to 1828. Then a young peasant, J. F. Millet, painted the country people and life near Cherbourg. By the mid-19th century, Eugène Boudin, son of an Honfleur river pilot, was painting seascapes and such superb skies that he was called 'King of the Skies'. He persuaded a young caricaturist, Claude Monet, to turn to painting and then persuaded the Honfleur authorities to sponsor Monet's studies in Paris.

At Ferme St-Siméon, just outside Honfleur, Boudin gath-ered round him young artists living in Normandy and their friends from Paris – Monet, Sisley, Brazille, Renoir, Pissarro, Cézanne. Their impassioned discussions over the farm cider led to the birth of Impressionism. All worked along this coast. They were nearly all desperately poor, too. Poor Sisley worked as a 'fishwife', gutting fish to find money to eat and to buy canvases. Ironic that now their paintings sell for such fortunes and the little cider house where they met is one of the most expensive hotels in Normandy.

In the Eugène Boudin Museum in Honfleur are works of several of the artists and also of Raoul Dufy (1877–1953) who came from Le Havre. There is a fine collection of his works in the André Malraux Museum in Le Havre. His work depicts the great years of tourism on the Normandy coast, showing con-

Gardens at Giverny

certs, regattas, racecourses, fashionable esplanades and beaches, in bright colours with a touch of humour.

Monet later lived just inside Normandy at Giverny where he painted the lilies in the pond of his superb old garden, now brilliantly restored.

Many of Normandy's lovely old buildings did survive even D-Day, and they are as much part of true Normandy as the apples and the cows in the lush meadows. The stone of which they are built was often quarried from the very land where the building stands. The ancient abbeys of Normandy are still a joy to visit.

The limestone of Caen was shipped to England after the Conquest to make some of Britain's finest buildings, including Westminster Abbey. The towers of Canterbury Cathedral are of Norman design. The style, developed by the Bénédictines, had pure lines, bold proportions but fairly simple decoration. It merged with the French Gothic in the 13th century, bringing more ornament and complication.

The Flamboyant Gothic style found its fulfilment in Rouen. Surprisingly, the stolid Normans took kindly to ornate Italian Renaissance styles in their homes, and there are still many big Renaissance stone mansions to be seen. But to Britons, Norman architecture is rustic. The black-and-white beamed farmhouses and cottages, many with thatched roofs, which abound from the Suisse-Normande to the Durdent valley and Bray countryside make a beautiful background to Normandy's cows and fruit trees.

Dieppe

[MAP 3, page 223]

For visitors arriving by ferry from Newhaven, Dieppe remains 'Instant France'. The scene and the atmosphere strike you immediately you step onto quai Henri IV as pure Norman. The fishing boats, the quayside fish market, the bistros and pavement cafés, the shops in Grand'Rue round the corner, are all part of the daily life of a busy port and commercial centre, not a tourist attraction. The big, grassy promenade and long beach are used for exercise by local people and their dogs, and Parisians too, for Dieppe has the nearest beach to Paris. Even the British tourists are part of the traditional scene. Boats ran regularly from Brighton in the 18th century and the Newhaven Packet was running a daily service by the 1850s. During the French Revolution, three Brighton masters of the Channel Packet Service – John Chapman and Samuel Barton father and son – ran a regular service for escaping aristocrats! But, unlike Boulogne, Dieppe does not have tourist invasions. There are fewer boats from Britain.

Although the commercial harbour is busy with boats bringing in cargoes ranging from timber from Scandinavia to exotic fruit and vegetables from Africa in which Dieppe has always specialised, and new factories in the outskirts make products from medical creams to Alpine Renault sports cars, fishing is still Dieppe's life blood. In the quayside market within a hundred metres of the ferry terminal fishwives sell miniature mussels, scallops, langouste, brill, shiny sole, John Dory, pink and brown shrimps and mullet while fishermen drink the salt out of their throats in the harbour cafés alongside Arcades de la Poissonerie and visitors sit inside and outside little restaurants consuming mountains of mussels, shrimps and whelks and lapping litres of wine at prices which would be a giveaway in Paris or Cannes. The fishing boats dock mostly at Le Pollet over the river bridge at Port de Pêche, where they mix with pleasure yachts, and it is on the quayside here that the fish market takes place early each morning.

Most fishermen live in the old Le Pollet quarter. It is interesting and photogenic.

The joy of Dieppe is Grand'Rue, most of it now for pedestrians only, with seats for weary window-shoppers. Individualistic shops are scattered higgledy-piggledy along both sides with a fashion boutique and a silversmith separated by an old-time grocer, trestle tables laden with chickens, cheese, butter and *pâtés* which have never seen a freezer; a children's clothes boutique with Paris styles next to a shop selling superb and interesting cooking pots, knives and ladles, and cone-shaped Chinois sieves, and fashion shoe shops alongside 'bar tabac'. In side streets are good bakers and food and wine shops, like l'Épicier Olivier in rue St Jacques, a grocer's with wine bargains stacked outside and gorgeous farm cheeses maturing in its cellar. It was started by the father of the great cheese expert Philippe Olivier of Boulogne and is still run by the family.

The Saturday morning market in Grand'Rue, spilling into rue St Jacques and rue St Jean, is splendid for food. The streets are packed with stalls offering farm-fresh products, barrels of butter, great terrines of farm-fresh pâté, sausages in scores of shapes and sizes, jumbo-size cheeses, little rounds of strong mature farm cheeses and big bowls of cream, alongside mounds of local vegetables and, at one end, barrows of fish and sometimes a whole barrow filled with little oysters at give-away prices. Three-fifths of the scallops (*coquilles St Jacques*) eaten in France are caught by Dieppe fishermen, and the shellfish and whitefish served in restaurants and bistros are superb. Dieppe is one of the best places in France to eat well at a reasonable price and to eat cheaply.

At the end of Grand'Rue is Café des Tribuneaux – an 18th-century inn, dark inside, often chaotic as waiters weave around tables and people. It has the atmosphere of an Impressionist painting of the 1880s in modern dress. Not surprising, for when they were not meeting in the studio of local painter and critic Jacques-Emile Blanche, who did not die until 1942, Renoir, Monet, Walter Sickert, James Whistler and the ageing Pissarro, whose painting of St Jacques Church is one of his greatest, were drifting in and out of the Tribuneaux. That was the 1880s. In the 1890s you would have seen in there the thin figure of Aubrey Beardsley, close to death, Henry Harland, editor of *The Yellow Book* for which Beardsley drew and which was considered so outrageous, and the greatest *Yellow Book* contributor, Oscar Wilde. Though dying in Dieppe in poverty and exile Oscar still had enough genius to write 'The Ballad of Reading Gaol'.

Tribuneaux is still the centre where students meet to argue, plan and sharpen their wits, as it has been for two hundred years.

An English colony almost took over Dieppe society around 1900. Its centre was the villa of Lord and Lady Cecil at Puys, and they imported British lifestyle and habits, from tea and kippers to Indian-Empire-style snobbery, treating most Dieppois as 'natives'. One Englishman was black-balled – the Prince of Wales, future Edward VII. He came over to see one of his mistresses, the Duchess of Caracciola, who had married her Neapolitan husband to get away from her parents and left him at the church door. The Prince was 'godfather' to her daughter Olga and visited them incognito in Dieppe. He gave Olga a seat at his coronation in Westminster Abbey. She married a baron and became a photographer for *Vogue*.

One member of the English set was the beautiful Lady Blanche Hozier, who was so addicted to gambling that she queued with sandwiches waiting for the Casino to open. One of her children, Clementine, became the wife of Winston Churchill and surprised General de Gaulle with her fluent French. That casino was flattened with the hotel alongside it by the Royal Navy during the 1942 Dieppe Raid. They were used as Nazi headquarters.

The new casino and Hotel Présidence are modern-style but many of the buildings along the Esplanade are still *fin-de-siècle* and many are still hotels. In summer parked cars now rather spoil the view of the grass-covered promenade, and there is a

swimming pool and beach restaurant in the middle but the
shingle beach looks much as it must have done when the English
imported the fashion for sea-bathing from Brighton. It was the
eccentric and flighty Duchesse de Berry who started the fashion
in Dieppe. Dominating the sea front is the castle built between
1435 and 1636, one of the very few buildings which survived an
English and Dutch naval bombardment in 1694 when the old
wooden town was demolished. The castle museum has models of
ships, navigation equipment and maps. One model is of *La
Dauphine*, in which Giovanni da Verrazzano sailed from Dieppe
to discover land which he proposed calling Angoulême Bay –
now known as New York. There is a fine collection of engravings
in the museum by Georges Braque, who lived nearby at Varangeville and there are works of Boudin, Pissarro, Sisley, Sickert, Blanche, Dufy and Jean Lurçat. The great exhibits are
intricate carvings in ivory, including boxes, sewing caskets, ships
in bottles and 19th-century sculptures by Pierre Graillon. This
art was developed in the 16th and 17th centuries when tusks
were landed from Africa and India. Once there were 300 ivory
carvers in Dieppe. Most were Protestants, and fled to Britain and
Holland after rights of religious freedom were revoked in
France. (The museum is closed on Tuesdays.)

In square du Canada below the castle is a monument to
Dieppe's New World explorers of the 16th to 18th centuries and
a plaque to the Canadians and Britons killed in the raid on Nazi
defences in August 1942. The idea of the Dieppe Raid was to
relieve Stalin (who was calling for a second front in the West) by
making the Germans keep up their western defences, and to test
methods of landing for the coming invasion. From a force of
5000 – 944 were killed including 697 Canadians and 229 British
and 18 other Allies. More than 600 were wounded and 1700
taken prisoner. The RAF lost 113 air crew. 28 tanks and over 90
aircraft were lost. 500 German soldiers were killed, 300 were
wounded and 48 aircraft were lost. Churchill called it 'recon-
naissance in depth'. Most historians agree that the experience
gained saved tens of thousands of lives in the 1944 Normandy
invasion. The British learned that they could not land vehicles
on a pebble beach and that they could not capture a port by
direct assault, but would need to create an artificial port. The

D-Day invasion might have failed without this knowledge. The Germans seem to have been lulled into a belief that they were safe if they held the ports. One unqualified success was by Lord Lovat's British Commandos, who landed at nearby Sainte Marguerite, achieved all their objectives, and got back. The cemetery for those killed in the raid is 3km away, off the Rouen road at St Aubin-sur-Scie. The raid is commemorated in Musée de Guerre, 2km west on D75 at a radar station which was a main target. It shows Allied and German tanks, vehicles and guns, and VI rockets fired by the Germans from Normandy at Britain in 1944. The museum, partly outdoors, is open 5 April–10 September.

The cathedral-sized St Jacques church, 12th century but considerably restored since, is an attractive mix-up of Flamboyant-Gothic and Renaissance styles and it has a 13th-century nave, 15th-century tower and an 18th-century dome. The frieze above the sacristy door shows a line of Brazilian Indians and commemorates the explorers of Dieppe. It was originally in Jean Ango's palace, which was of wood and destroyed in the 1694 bombardment.

Almost anything old in Dieppe is connected with Jean Ango, a 16th-century shipbuilder and privateer who became Governor of Dieppe. In France, Ango is regarded rather as the British regard Sir Francis Drake, but he was a pirate to the English and especially to the Portuguese. He attacked and captured more than 300 Portuguese merchant ships. Then he retired to his palace of wood in Dieppe and a most interesting country mansion 8km away near Varangeville (*see* below). He lent a fortune to Francois I and died poor and forgotten. Ango is buried in St Jacques church in a chapel which he built. Manoir d'Ango (south of Dieppe, off D75) was built for Ango by Italian Renaissance craftsmen. The huge arcaded courtyard surrounded by steep-roofed buildings has an ornate dovecote, combining brick, flint and sandstone (open 1 April to early November).

At Château Miromesnil (8km south of Dieppe at Jouville-sur-Arques) the writer Guy de Maupassant is said to have been born in 1850. In fact he was born in Fécamp, but his mother moved him immediately to the Château so he would be registered from a posh address. On the edge of the splendid park is a statue to him. The château is 17th century and was once the house of the Marquis Hue de Miromesnil, Minister to Louis XVI. The church dates from 1517, belonging to a château destroyed after the battle in 1589 at nearby Arques, where Henri IV won a magnificent victory with 7000 Protestants over 30,000 Catholics of the extremist Catholic League led by the Duc de Mayenne, brother of the League's founder, the notorious Duc de Guise. The stained-glass windows of the church range from 1583 to modern works of 1964 by Guy de Voguë and by Charles Mareq, brilliant restorer of Reims Cathedral.

Puys, 4km east of Dieppe, now virtually a suburb with Dieppe's second beach, was discovered in 1868 by George Sand. She recommended it to the younger Alexandre Dumas who built a manor here which became a centre for writers and artists. His father Alexandre Dumas, writer of the great French historical novels, came here to die, almost broke after running through two fortunes. Claude Debussy passed summers in Puys and composed 'L'Isle Heureuse' there. Puys became the centre of the British colony in Dieppe.

For other places close to Dieppe, see Pourville, Varangeville, Ste Marguerite-sur-Mer, Offranville, Arques-la-Bataille.

TOURIST INFORMATION 1 boul. du Gén-de-Gaulle
(35.84.11.77 – shut Sunday)
MARKETS Saturday in Grand'Rue and surrounds.
Smaller markets Tuesday, Wednesday, Thursday
FESTIVALS carnival around 15 August; herrring festival
– November

HOTELS

La Présidence, 1 boul. Verdun (35.84.31.31): comfortable, modern. Restaurant on fourth floor. ROOMS E–G. MEALS C–F.
L'Univers, 10 boul. Verdun (35.84.12.55): Jean Tilquin cooks Norman dishes superbly, especially local fish. We have enjoyed his meals for thirty-six years. Old-style, comfortable family

hotel, slightly eccentric but fun. ROOMS E–F. MEALS C–F. Shut 10 December–1 February.

Arcades, 1 Arcade de la Bourse (35.84.14.12): much improved in efficiency and especially food. ROOMS C–E. MEALS C–F.

RESTAURANTS

Marmite Dieppoise, 8 rue St-Jean (35.84.24.26): still the place to taste superb fish cooked the old Norman way. *Marmite dieppoise* is a Norman soup-stew of fish and shellfish, with leeks, wine and cream. Try Jean-Pierre Toussat's *sole normande* and chicken in cider. Gastronomic menu is superb. MEALS C–F. Shut Thursday and Sunday evenings and Monday; 20 June–15 July; 15–31 October.

La Mélie, 2 Grande rue Pollet (35.84.21.19): in old fishermen's quarter, where patron-chef Guy Brachais moved from Tocqueville-sur-Eu. Good delicate cooking of fish. Try *creuille de pêcheur* (small pieces of fish beautifully poached). Good lamb fillets in garlic cream, too. MEALS C–F. Shut Monday, Sunday evening; November, February.

Moderne, 21 arcades Poissonnerie (35.84.66.90): two storeys with harbour views at the top. No fast food here – Norman dishes mostly cooked to order. Good *marmite dieppoise*. MEALS B–E.

In the row of old-style little restaurants along quai Henri IV by the ferry terminal, these are long-standing favourites:

Du Port, 99 quai Henri IV (35.84.36.64): used by locals and tourists. Busy. Good value. Try *coquilles St Jacques* (scallops) *à la dieppoise*. MEALS A–C, F. Shut early January–early February.

Sully, 97 quai Henri IV (35.84.23.13): MEALS A–G. Shut Tuesday evening, Wednesday.

L'Armorique, 17 quai Henri IV (35.84.28.14): for fish-meals, one-dish snacks such as oysters, take-away cooked dishes (like fish soup, *moules marinières*) or take-away fresh fish including shellfish direct from local boats. MEALS (*à la carte*) D–G. Shut Monday, Sunday evening; 1–15 June, 15–31 October.

At Vertus, 7km south on N27

La Bûcherie, route de Rouen (35.84.83.10): smart, shiny, fashion-able, with cocktail bar. Pricey, but excellent classic cuisine, from marmite and lobster to apple tart. MEALS D–G. Shut Monday, Sunday evening; 15–25 January, 15–30 September.

At Martin-Eglise, 6km south-east on D1

Clos Normand, 22 rue Henri IV (35.82.71.01): charming 15th-century auberge. Bedrooms (for diners only) improved. Reliable old-style Norman cooking (duck with apples, mussel tart, turbot in cream sauce) by Regis Hauchecomer. ROOMS D–E. MEALS D–F. Shut Monday evening, Tuesday; 15 December–15 January.

Rouen

[MAP 3, page 223]

As we entered Rouen down a hill we met a 'T' junction. 'Toutes Directions' said the sign to the left. 'Autres Directions' said the right-hand sign.

That seems to sum up Rouen's split personality. Though much rebuilt after the 1940 burning and the 1944 bombing, the old city of spires and belltowers is romantically beautiful, even when crammed with summer visitors. The new industrial city, a pride of the new 'Technological France', is such a concrete mess of ugly flyovers and aggressively utilitarian factories, that surely no-one could love it but a company accountant gloating over a balance sheet. But that is where Rouen finds its wealth and prosperity.

Rouen is built in a loop in the Seine and much is made of the fact that wartime bombing allowed planners to move all the factories on the left bank to the outskirts and build a modern residential area near the river. Alas, the chance was missed to make the residential area attractive, let alone beautiful. But the old centre of the city was sympathetically restored, though some changes are not really compatible.

Rouen is well worth exploring and, as with all old cities with narrow lanes, you must do it on foot. Parts of the old city are now only open to pedestrians. You might even be able to park beside Place du Vieux Marché, the old market, where Joan of Arc was burned in 1431. That is the usual centre for exploration.

This square is surrounded by fine houses of the 16th–18th centuries, many black-and-white timbered. In the middle are three modern structures by Louis Arretche claimed by the French guides 'to fit masterfully into the architectural vision of the Place'. Well ... the market is airy and a great place for buying cheese. The great twenty-metre-high concrete cross on the spot where Joan died, La Croix de Réhabilitation, is a national monument but not a great work of art. The daring modern Jeanne d'Arc church, finished in 1979 and clad in grey slate and bright copper to symbolise the ash and flames of her

Rouen

burning, is a fine and imaginative modern building, but it is in
the wrong place architecturally. It would have looked splendid
on the campus of the new and modern university on the other
river bank. One of its delights is the way that the architect fitted
in the lovely 16th-century stained glass windows rescued from
the bombed Saint Vincent church. Eastward from the square is
the delightful Rue du Gros-Horloge, a lovely, busy old shopping
street lined with half-timbered buildings dating back to the 14th
century. Its masterpiece is the Gros Horloge, the superb Renaissance clock with a golden face on each side which spans the
street on a bridge. It is a symbol of Rouen. Beside it is a 14th-
century belfry which rings its bell daily at 9 a.m., the time of the
ancient curfew. Climb the stairs to the roof for a splendid panorama of the old city of spires and towers.

At the far end of Rue du Gros-Horloge is the cathedral of
Notre-Dame, built between 1145 and 1514, and one of the
greatest Gothic buildings in the world. Monet was almost
obsessed with painting its rich façade of charming variety. The
great cast-iron steeple (152 metres high) which dominates its
silhouette was not added until the 19th century. Between the
simple 12th-century early-Gothic St Romain tower and sumptu-
ously flamboyant 15th-century Tour de Beurre, paid for by rich
citizens in return for a Papal dispensation to allow them to eat
Normandy butter during Lent, the huge façade is rich in open
tracery, broken by huge doorways. It is this west façade which
Monet painted so often at different times of day to show the
effect of different light. The delicate carving of the archways
and tympana and the flamboyant latticework window galleries
over the doors are sheer delight. But the finest doorway is along
the north side off the Cour des Libraires – Portail des Libraires
(the Booksellers' doorway).

Inside the cathedral is of harmonious simplicity but contains
some superb windows and beautiful ornate tombs. The early
Gothic double-storeyed nave is dominated by a bold lantern
tower 51 metres high, supported by great groups of columns. In
the north arm of the transept is a large attractive rose window
restored with its original 14th-century glass.

The chancel is simple, noble and beautiful. 15th-century
stained glass windows depict Calvary while the Joan of Arc

chapel has modern windows by the great Max Ingrand. The modern altar is of a marble slab from Aosta in Italy with an 18th-century Christ in gilded lead by Clodion. In the ambulatory behind the altar are recumbent tombs of Rollo, first Duke of Normandy, his son William Longsword, Henry the Young King (second son of Henry II of England) and his heroic brother Richard Lionheart (King Richard I of England). The tomb contains only his heart with a Latin inscription. In the chapel behind is the splendidly ornate monumental Renaissance tomb by Roulland le Roux (1515) showing supposed cardinal virtues (justice, strength, temperance and prudence) and the three theological virtues (faith, hope and charity). It is a fitting memorial to the Amboises, for one of them really introduced Italian Renaissance to French building. The other tomb, by Jean Goujon, is of Louis de Brézé (1535) Seneschal of Normandy and husband of the beautiful and dignified Diane de Poitiers, widowed at 32, mistress of Henri II of France.

Behind the cathedral is a striking 15th-century Flamboyant Gothic church St Maclou, much restored after 1944 damage. Two doorways have superb Renaissance panels, probably by Jean Goujon. The nearby cloister (Aître St Maclou) is a mediaeval plague cemetery, with carvings of gravediggers' tools and the Danse Macabre. It now houses the School of Fine Arts. Rue Damiette from St Maclou church is lined with beautiful old half-timbered houses, many now antique shops. You get a fine view of Rouen's other magnificent imposing church, the abbey church of St Ouen, with a huge and delightful lantern tower looming over the old town, great high windows with 14th-century stained glass and one of the biggest organs in France.

The Palais de Justice, a superb blend of Renaissance and Flamboyant Gothic architecture was damaged in 1944, and during rebuilding a 12th-century synagogue was found, one of the oldest in Europe.

Rouen is rich in good museums. Musée des Beaux-Arts is very big and has important works from many great artists (Place Verdrel, rue Thiers – Open 10–12 a.m., 2–6 p.m.; shut Tuesday, Wednesday morning). They include possibly the greatest Flemish primitive painting *The Virgin and the Saints* by Gérard

David (1523); Italian, Spanish and French 18th-century paintings; masterpieces by Nicolas Poussin, Caravaggio, Rubens,
Ingres, Velasquez, Fragonard, and a mainly Impressionist room
with paintings by Sisley, Renoir, Dufy and Monet, including one
of his paintings of Rouen Cathedral. Another room is devoted to
a local artist Jacques-Emile Blanche (1861–1942), a portraitist of
leading writers, musicians and intellectuals. Here are interesting
paintings of André Gide, Cocteau, Stravinsky, André Maurois,
Mauriac and Paul Valéry. The Cubist avant-garde local painters
of the early 20th century, the Duchamps have a small exhibition,
including Marcel Duchamp's 'Boîte en Valise', a small-scale
reconstruction of his works in a suitcase!

Near this museum, in a lovely 17th-century house of the
Hocqueville family at 1 rue Faucon, is a most interesting Cer-
amic Museum (Musée de la Céramique) showing 6000 pieces of
French or foreign china and glass (same opening hours as
Beaux-Arts). Most interesting are richly ornamented Rouen
china of Louis XIV and XV periods. These kings used china
after melting down gold and silver plate to pay for wars. Musée
le Secq des Tournelles in the former church of St Laurent shows
12,000 objects in wrought iron, from keys to grills (same
opening hours as Beaux-Arts). Musée des Antiquités de la Seine-
Maritime, 198 rue Beauvoisins in the former convent of St
Marie (1630) shows many old treasures, including carved
ivories, Renaissance tapestries, glass and furniture from prehis-
tory to the 19th century (shut Sundays and Mondays).

Gustave Flaubert, the writer, was born in Rouen in 1821 but
was not loved there in his lifetime. The citizens even prayed for
his punishment when he was being prosecuted for the
'immorality' of *Madame Bovary*. He had been very rude about
their narrow-mindedness. His birthplace, part of the 17th-
century Hôtel Dieu (church hospital) at 51 rue Lecat, has family
furniture and documents but is also a medical museum. His
father was a surgeon here. Rouen looked more kindly on the
great dramatist Pierre Corneille, born there in 1606. A *lycée* in
the 17th-century Jesuit College where he studied is named after
him. Cavelier La Salle, the explorer, Flaubert, Guy de Maupassant and André Maurois all studied there. Quite a school. There
is a museum of Corneille's family at his house, Manoir Pierre

Corneille, at Petit-Couronne, 8km SW of Rouen on the Le Mans–Elbeuf road N138.

TOURIST INFORMATION place de la Cathédrale, tel. 35.71.41.77
MARKET DAYS Tuesday, Wednesday, Friday, Saturday at market halls, place Vieux Marché
FESTIVALS May (Sunday nearest to 30th): Fêtes de Jeanne d'Arc. November – St Romain's Fair

HOTELS

Dieppe and *Restaurant Les Quatre Saisons*, place Bernard-Tissot (35.71.96.00); unless you are rich and love nouvelle cuisine, a good place to stay and eat – as it has been since my youth. Rooms recently redecorated and soundproofed. Classic Norman dishes, from *sole normande* (which I first learned to cook here) to *canard à la rouennaise* just as the hotel prepared and cooked it for King Edward VII on one of his dinner excursions during a passionate weekend in Dieppe! ROOMS E–F. MEALS D–F.

RESTAURANTS

Gill, 60 rue St Nicolas (35.71.16.14): I am told that thirty-year-old Gilles Tournadre is one of the great chefs of the future. Very light dishes, it seems, but very expensive. With his popularity and complicated closing times, I have been unable to taste his cooking. MEALS G. Shut 22 August–13 September; part February; Monday (except evening in summer), Sunday.
Bertrand Warin, 7–9 rue de la Pie (35.89.26.69). Former pupil of the great Guérard who introduced the slimmers' *cuisine minceur*, so light, modern cooking, over-priced except at lunchtime. Beautiful Norman décor. MEALS C (lunch), G. Shut 3 weeks August; Monday, Sunday (except lunch September–June).
Le Beffroy, 15 rue Beffroy (35.71.55.27): Dorothée l'Hernault from Dusseldorf, an adopted Norman, cooks fine *marmite dieppoise*, *lotte vallée d'Auge, canard Duclair* and serves superb Norman

farm-made cheeses as well as some Provençal and modern
dishes. Worth visiting. MEALS D (weekday lunch), F–G. Shut 26
July–mid-August; mid–end February; Sunday, Monday.
La Cache-Ribaud, 10 rue du Tambour (35.71.04.82): good, old
regional dishes at sensible prices. MEALS A–E. Shut Sunday
except in summer.

Around place du Vieux Marché are many bistros. Popular *La
Couronne* ('oldest auberge in France') is now pretentious and
touristy. Le Bouchon de Rouen is too expensive. Try these:
Les Halles du Vieux Marché, 41 place du Vieux Marché
(35.71.03.58): old-style cooking, quick service; cheap. MEALS
A–C.
Les Maraîchers, 37 place du Vieux Marché (35.71.57.73): new
bistro with old-style cooking of local ingredients. Good local
meat. Excellent value. MEALS A–C.
Vieux Logis, near Hôtel de Ville, 8 rue Joyeuse (35.71.55.30):
small bistro; one incredibly cheap menu, including wine (55F in
1988!) Open every day.

At Val-de-la-Haye (10km SW by D51)
Auberge La Muserolle, 15 quai Napoleon (35.32.40.85): lovely old
Norman house (1610) beside Seine, old hunting inn. Delicious
cooking of regional dishes (Norman and Flemish).

Le Havre

[MAP 3, page 223]

I saw Le Havre in 1946 truly flattened from the war – total
desolation. Even the street surfaces around the docks had been
destroyed by bombs and flame-throwers and the only bar in
sight was in the cellar of a wrecked building. It was Europe's

mu aged ot. ow t s

worst damaged port. Now it is the second biggest port in France to Marseilles, a commercial centre rather than a tourist centre. The only signposts from the ferry quay where P&O boats from Portsmouth dock lead you straight out of town. The whole town was replanned by a man who believed that reinforced concrete is beautiful – Auguste Perret (1874–1954), teacher of Le Corbusier. It is the antithesis of the old Le Havre, with its ancient houses, little bistros, narrow streets and blind alleys. Le Havre today is either a masterpiece of modern planning or a soul-less, unappealing, cold concrete jungle, according to your viewpoint. It has some undoubted advantages.

The arcades are useful for window-shopping in wet or cold weather. Avenue Foch, designed to be a modern Champs-Elysées, has shops as smart, interesting and as expensive as Paris. Perret's huge church of St Joseph, with a tower 109 metres tall which looks like a rocket on a launching pad and is a useful landmark if you get lost among the concrete, is sombre from without but warm within, with colour from the mosaic of narrow slabs of stained glass in the tower and walls. The vaulting is 80 metres high. The enormous Place de l'Hôtel de Ville, one of the biggest squares in Europe, is still dominated by Perret's lengthy town hall (108 metres) with a 17-storey concrete tower 72 metres high. Behind the town hall is a more interesting modern building – a church and belltower designed by Henri Colbosc in 1964. The major road opposite was rue de Paris before the war, an attractive street of 18th-century houses. The modern Bourse is in grey-granite. A new cultural centre in place Gambetta has concert halls, a theatre and conference centre under flattish igloos.

One new building which looks functional and plain but is almost perfect for its function is the Musée de Beaux-Arts Malraux. It is worth tarrying in Le Havre just to browse around it. Built of glass, aluminium and steel with huge windows towards the sea, it is ideal for showing paintings in almost any light. It contains an extensive and very fine collection from the 16th century to the present. Among its treasures are pictures by lesser-known but highly important 19th- and 20th-century artists such as Géricault, Michel, J. B. Corot and Fantin-Latour. Much is devoted to Impressionists and Post-Impressionists.

There are three hundred works of Eugène Boudin (see page
20); the collection was presented in 1900 by Boudin's brother.
There are four paintings by Monet, Boudin's protégé, including
the superb *Towers of Westminster* (1903) and seventy works by
Raoul Dufy.

There are some fine paintings of Normandy – Boudin's
paintings of Deauville, Trouville and Etretat, Dufy's horse-
racing scenes at Deauville and scenes of Le Havre; also Pissarro's
Bateaux à Honfleur and Monet's *Falaises à Varangeville*.

The Beaux-Arts Malraux is closed on Tuesdays.

In contrast, the Musée de l'Ancien Havre is housed appro-
priately in a 17th-century timber-framed house which escaped
war damage. It is in rue Delavigne alongside Bassin de la Barre
and is closed on Mondays and Tuesdays. The museum has
documents, plans and engravings from the town's foundation in
1517 to the end of the 19th century, model ships, glass and
Eastern porcelain.

Le Havre was planned as a port in 1517 by Francois I
because the old port of Harfleur was silted up. It was to be called
Franciscopolis. A name like that was courting the wrath of the
gods, which came in the form of a freak tide which collapsed its
walls. So an Italian refugee engineer, Bellarmato, showed the
French how to build on tidal mud – perhaps he had studied in
Venice. Le Havre grew rich as the port for supplying the Americans in the War of Independence. In 1864 one of the first
transatlantic steamers, the *Washington*, sailed between Le Havre
and New York.

Harfleur, 6km east, was founded as a port called Cara-
cotinum by the Romans. Its importance to the English and
French in the Hundred Years War led to constant fighting and
destruction but it died from river Seine silt and is now in the
heart of Le Havre's spreading industrial zone. You can see from
afar the spire of its lovely Flamboyant church St Martin (15th–
16th centuries).

The snobbier and elegant suburb of Le Havre is Ste
Adresse, seat of the Belgian Government in the 1914–18 War,
with a resort and old town built on terraces up the steep slope of
Cape Hève. There are wide views of Le Havre and the estuary

from a terrace reached by stairs, and good restaurants. A more pleasant place for an overnight stay than Le Havre itself.

Between Easter and mid-September, boat trips around the port leave from Le Havre yacht harbour. Other excursion boats go up the Seine to Villequier and Rouen, and from Le Havre to Honfleur and Deauville.

TOURIST INFORMATION 1 place de l'Hôtel de Ville, tel. 35.21.22.88. Closed Sunday
MARKET DAYS Tuesday, Thursday, Saturday
FESTIVALS Early July – sea festival. July – big international regatta. Sunday after 15 August – flower festival (Corso Fleurie)

HOTELS

Bordeaux, 147 rue Louis Brindeau (35.22.69.44): no restaurant. New, comfortable; town centre. ROOMS E–F.

At Ste Adresse
Phares, 29 rue Gén. de Gaulle (35.46.31.86): friendly family-run B-and-B hotel in old house with modern annexe. ROOMS B–D. Shut 24 December–2 January.
Monaco, 16 rue Paris (35.42.21.01): Max Lucas's classic cooking is delightful. Superb Duclair duck, home-smoked salmon. MEALS C (weekdays),D,G (restaurant shut Monday, from Oct–May). ROOMS B–E (shut 14–18 Feb).

RESTAURANTS

La Chaumette, 17 rue Racine (35.43.66.80); Christine Frechet's fish dishes are especially superb – local fish, absolutely fresh (nothing frozen) cooked for you, so it is no good trying to hurry. Excellent brioches filled with mussels, egg in red pepper jelly! Vegetables fresh from the market. Rather pricey. MEALS E–G.

Shut Saturday lunch, Sunday; Easter; fifteen days in August; 22
December–2 January.
Huitrière, 4 rue Paris (35.21.48.48): near P&O ferry terminal.
Fish only. Good stuffed oysters; mussel dishes. MEALS C–D.
Shut Monday.

At Ste Adresse

Yves Page, 7 place Clémenceau (35.46.06.09): good fresh fish;
lobster tank. Superb sea views from terrace. MEALS D–G (dégus-
tation). Shut 10 August–2 September; Sunday evening,
Monday.
Beau Séjour, 3 place Clémenceau (35.46.19.69): another with
good fish, lobster tank, sea views. Also excellent pâtisserie. Air-
conditioned. MEALS C (weekends)–G. Open all year.
Nice-Havrais, 6 place Fréderic-Sauvage (35.46.14.59): splendid
views, pleasant service, good cooking including some unusual
creations (cold turbot soufflé with green-pea sauce; duck with
tropical fruits and lavender honey). MEALS E, G. Shut Sunday
and Monday evenings.

Caen

[MAP 6, page 226]

Three-quarters of Caen was destroyed in 1944. Because it is
joined to the sea by a 12km canal to Ouistreham, built in the
19th century, the Allies regarded it as such an important port
that they made it their first prime target. The battle between the
Canadians and Germans lasted from 9–20 July, leaving devastation. Happily, rebuilding was sympathetic and well planned.

Abbaye aux Hommes

Historically important buildings were carefully restored. New buildings are made of the beautiful creamy Caen stone which centuries ago was exported to build the Tower of London and Canterbury Cathedral. It is a modern industrial city but is pleasant enough. Its prosperity has made it a centre of good shopping and good food. Recently the industrial area has spread without restraint.

Caen remains the city of William the Conqueror. The Pope had excommunicated him for marrying his cousin Matilda, but his adviser Lanfranc, an Italian monk from the Bec-Hellouin abbey, interceded with Pope Alexander II who was one of Lanfranc's old pupils. As a penance William founded the Abbaye aux Hommes in Caen and Matilda founded the Abbaye aux Dames. Both were paid for with booty stolen from England.

Matilda was Regent of Normandy while William was away conquering England, and was crowned Queen of England in 1068. She was buried in her Caen abbey in 1087. Meanwhile Willian made Lanfranc Archbishop of Canterbury and ruler of

England while William was in Normandy. William was buried in the Abbaye aux Hommes. Both abbeys have survived many attacks, including a sacking by Edward III of England in 1346 and by the English troops of Henry V in 1417. Henry repaired the damage to Caen and the English ruled it for 33 years. In 1432 the Duke of Bedford, Henry VI of England's regent in Normandy, founded Caen University. It was the first in France.

The church of William's abbey, St Étienne, was altered in the 13th century and they added a superb Gothic east end with superimposed turrets and flying buttresses. A marble slab marks the Conqueror's tomb though his bones were scattered during the Revolution.

From D-Day in 1944, for three days and nights, hundreds of people hid in the church and abbey buildings and remained unhurt while Caen collapsed around them. The French regarded this as a miracle, and if local legend is true, so should loyal Englishmen, for it has been said for centuries that the English crown will last as long as St Étienne's stands.

Matilda's abbey church is Romanesque except for a 13th-century chapel in the transept. The two west towers lost their spires in the Hundred Years War and were replaced by an incongruous balustrade. The huge nave with nine bays is pure Romanesque. Matilda's tomb is in the chancel – a slab of black marble set there in 1083. The other abbey buildings, rebuilt in the 17th century, were badly damaged in 1944.

Caen has many churches. St Nicolas (now deconsecrated) is particularly interesting as it has never been altered since it was built by the monks of the Abbaye aux Hommes in the 11th century. The Romanesque door is lovely.

The St Jean quarter of Caen was almost totally destroyed in 1944 but St Jean church has been rebuilt. Flamboyant Gothic, it was built originally in the 14th and 15th centuries, its rich decoration paid for by rich merchants. In the place de la Résistance nearby is a statue of Joan of Arc, sent back from Oran by the Algerians after they gained independence from France.

The castle, with ramparts from William's time, was enlarged over centuries. It looks impressive on its spur of rock, despite wartime damage. In a modern building in the grounds is the Musée des Beaux-Arts with a collection of fine paintings strong in 16th- and 17th-century works. It has Napoleon to thank for its fine collections of Italian, Dutch and Flemish paintings. His armies looted them. So did his uncle, Cardinal Fesch. Then in 1872 Bernard Mancel's collection was added, with superb prints by such masters as Mantegna, Dürer, Rembrandt, Callot and Goya. Among Napoleon's booty is Perugino's *Marriage of the Virgin*. There are 16th-century works of the Breughels and Veronese, a fine Portrait of a Woman by the Dutchman Frans Floris. 17th-century works include Rubens and Poussin's beautiful *Death of Adonis*. Furniture and ceramics are excellent, too. (Open in summer 10 a.m.–noon, 2–6 p.m.; winter 2–5 p.m. Closed Tuesday).

Musée de Normandie is in the old Governor's house of the château. It is more interesting than most local history museums, with tools used in Norman households and on farms (same opening hours as Beaux-Arts).

Some of Caen's old buildings which survived wartime destruction are at the foot of the castle, including an early Renaissance mansion Hôtel d'Escoville (1 place Pierre) built by a rich merchant around 1535. It is now the Tourist Office. Other old houses are in place St Sauveur and rue aux Fromages leading to it. St Sauveur's church, an unusual mixture of Gothic and Renaissance, recalls the former nuns of St Sauveur who nursed a sick, destitute and demented Englishman until his death in 1840. He was Beau Brummell, once arbiter of all fashion and elegance from clothes to etiquette and virtual dictator at Bath and Tunbridge Wells in their heydays. Alas, his wit was too barbed for the Prince Regent, his gambling debts grew, and he fled to Paris. In 1830 he was granted a sinecure as British consul in Caen but was made redundant in 1832. French friends rescued him from a debtors' prison and he lived in the now-departed Hotel Angleterre, planning and sending out invitations for elegant parties to which no one turned up.

Musée de la Poste et Communication, 52 rue St Pierre, follows interestingly the history of post, telegraph and telephones, with stamps, horse-drawn mail coaches and early instruments (shut Tuesday, Saturday in winter).

The new university covers eighty acres with rather utilitarian buildings. There are 12,000 students now. The Duke of Bedford who started it in 1432 probably had something more like the dreaming spires of Oxford in mind. See also: D-Day beaches – (Bénouville, Pegasus Bridge 10km).

TOURIST INFORMATION 1 place St Pierre tel. 31.86.27.65
MARKET DAYS every day except Monday. Local markets include St Sauveur (Friday), St Pierre (Sunday), Cygne de Croix (Wednesday and Saturday), Chemin d'Authie (Tuesday, Thursday).
FESTIVALS June–antiques show; September–Caen Fair with horse-racing

HOTELS

Relais des Gourmets, 15 rue de Geôle (31.86.06.01), comfortable with pricey restaurant (traditional cooking). ROOMS D–G. MEALS F,G. Shut Sunday evening.
Moderne, 116 boul. Mar-Leclerc (31.86.04.23). Mapotel with elegant restaurant Les Quatre Vents serving good-value meals; good fish; Normandy cheeses. ROOMS C–F. MEALS B–F (restaurant shut Sunday evening in winter).

RESTAURANTS WITH ROOMS

Le Dauphin, 29 rue Gémare (31.86.22.26): Robert Charbedier's Norman country dishes have devotees from all over France and Britain. In old priory near castle. Nice small bedrooms. ROOMS D–F. MEALS A (weekdays), B–G (restaurant shut Saturday). Shut part February; mid-July to mid-August.

At Bénouville, 10km north-west
Manoir d'Hastings et La Pommeraie (31.44.62.43): in my opinion, Claude Scaviner is still the best chef in this area. He makes superb use of all Normandy's delicious ingredients in traditional regional dishes and his own versions. And his son Yves is almost as good. Fine service, excellent wine stocks. 'Winter garden' bar.

All in 7th-century Norman priory beside historic Pegasus Bridge (see D-Day Beaches – page 57). Eleven attractive, pricey rooms for those who have wined and dined well. Book! ROOMS G. MEALS E–G. Shut 1–15 February.

At Bavent 8km south-east Caen
Host. du Moulin du Ré, (31.78.83.68): prettily converted old mill by a park with lake. Attractive bedrooms. Delicious light dishes of farm-fresh food. Meals rather pricey. ROOMS D. MEALS F. Shut 1–15 March; 1–31 October; restaurant shut Sunday evening, Monday except July, August.

RESTAURANTS

Echevins, 35 route Trouville (31.84.10.17): local favourite. Patrick Regnier (ex-Benoit, Paris, Oasis, Napoule and Tour d'Argent) has moved to an 1882 manor house. Superb fish. Choice of classic or modern dishes. MEALS D–G. Shut Sunday, part February and early July.
La Bourride, 15 rue Vaugueux (31.93.50.76), in 17th-century house in Caen's old quarter. Norman regional and modern cuisine, with no excesses. Dear but worth the money. Speciality – *bourride!* (white fish stew thickened with garlic mayonnaise). MEALS F–G. Shut Sunday, Monday; 15–30 August; 3–24 January.
Relais Normandy, place de la Gare (31.82.24.58): one of France's best station buffets and restaurants. Renowned for 20 years. Regional cooking. MEALS A–D.
L'Ecaille, 13 rue de Geôle (31.86.49.10): fish and shellfish only – locals say the best shellfish in Caen. MEALS C. Shut Saturday lunch.

Bayeux

[MAP 6, page 226]

Bayeux is a treasure of a town. Because it is both delightful and interesting, it can become crowded from Easter to early autumn, but traffic, which used to rather spoil it, is now banned from the very centre.

Pliny mentioned it as a Gaulish city in AD 50 and by the 3rd century it was a walled town with temples, public baths and a well-known college for Druids on the banks of the Aure river. The Bretons took it, then the Saxons, and finally the Norseman Rollo who founded the line of Norman Dukes by marrying the Governor of Bayeux's daughter Popa. It was in Bayeux that the Saxon Harold, to get his freedom to return to England, made his fatal oath of allegiance to Duke William, leading to the Norman conquest of England. Even when the French took over Rouen in the 15th century Bayeux remained staunchly Scandinavian and the people continued to speak Norse!

Bayeux's memorial plaque to the British 50th Northumberland Division is well deserved. Their highly successful land-

Bayeux tapestry

ing on D-Day at Gold Beach and quick overpowering of German opposition enabled them to free Bayeux the next day, almost unscathed. It was the first town in France to be freed and the luckiest in Normandy. All the rest were badly damaged.

As miraculous as the survival of Bayeux in 1944 is the survival of the Bayeux tapestry. It is not really a tapestry but an enormous piece of coloured embroidery on wool, a seventy-metre-long strip divided into many scenes telling not just the story of the Conquest of England but the whole story from Harold's shipwreck, his promise to renounce the crown of England in favour of William, his refusal and William's invasion of England. It is all told as Norman propaganda, of course, stressing William's 'right' to the English throne. The Normans are clean-cut and clean shaven, the sinister Saxons have drooping moustaches. The restrained colours of red, blue, green and grey on natural-coloured wool have survived since the 11th century, possibly because the tapestry was rolled up in a trunk for centuries. Napoleon took it to Paris to whip up support for his own planned invasion of England.

In the 18th century, the tapestry was suddenly attributed to William's Queen Matilda. It is usually called the Queen's Tapestry still in France. Its original name was Telle du Conquest. It was almost certainly commissioned in England by the Conqueror's warlike half-brother Odo, who was both Bishop of Bayeux and Count of Kent, and was made by the already-famous Anglo-Saxon embroiderers over ten years. It was originally hung round the apse of Bayeux Cathedral. Now it is shown splendidly in the 17th-century house, excellently lit and protected by glass. You can hire a tape in French or English to explain it. (Museum shut 25 December and 1 January). The centre strip of the embroidery relates the main story. The upper and lower bands show scenes from Aesop's fables and from everyday Norman life of the times, some fairly explicitly erotic.

The Baron Gérard museum across the square in the old Bishop's Palace, has some good porcelain from Bayeux and Valognes, fine old and new Bayeux lace, and a mixed but good collection of paintings including local artists, primitives, French Impressionist and modern paintings (shut 25 December and 1 January).

Bayeux Cathedral is one of the finest in France – a really stunning building but slightly hemmed in. Typically Gothic, it was built between 1055 and 1077. The central tower is 15th century with the top added in the 19th century. The tympanum, rather worn, tells the story of the murder of Thomas à Becket at Canterbury.

I love the Romanesque and Gothic blend of the interior, with its impressive tall windows and 13th-century vaulting, its superb Romanesque nave, and funny grotesque carvings on arches between the columns.

Bayeux has some fine, old houses and an attractive coaching inn called the Lion d'Or, accustomed to welcoming everyone who comes to see the tapestry, from passing tourists to the grand

14th-century half-timbered house, the oldest in Bayeux

and famous. A very modern memorial museum of the Battle of Normandy, with tanks outside on guard, is divided into exhibits of the British and American forces. (Open daily except November–February, when it opens Saturday and Sunday).

In the castle park of the small market town of Creully overlooking the Seulles valley (14km E of Bayeux) General Montgomery, Commander-in-Chief of ground forces in the invasion, set up his headquarters in June 1944 in the same caravan he had used in the successful Battle of Alamein in the north African desert. The castle (11th–12th century) has a separate 16th-century round turret (open July, August) and a Romanesque-Gothic church with 17th century belfry.

TOURIST INFORMATION 1 rue Cuisiniers (31.92.16.26)
MARKET every afternoon

HOTELS

Lion d'Or, 71 rue St Jean (31.92.06.90): founded 1770 as coaching inn. In city centre, it is set back in courtyard, so it is a Relais du Silence. Very well run; fine Norman cooking. ROOMS C–F. MEALS C–G. Shut 20 December–20 January.
Argouges, 21 rue St Patrice (31.92.88.86): no restaurant; in charming 18th-century house. ROOMS D–F.
Luxembourg et Quatre Saisons, 25 rue des Bouchers (31.92.00.04): fairly luxurious hotel made from an old Relais de Poste; good restaurant with variety of dishes and menu prices. Rooms E–G. MEALS D–G. Open every day all year.

RESTAURANT

Taverne des Ducs, 4 place St Patrice (31.92.09.88): tavern and brasserie in town centre open until midnight. MEALS D–F. Open all year.

Cherbourg

[MAP 7, page 227]

Cherbourg is very much a man-created port which had two great periods of glory. The first was in the 1930s when the big fashionable Atlantic liners docked here and the great sight of Cherbourg was watching the rich, famous and notorious coming and going aboard the great boats, like *Ile de France, Queen Mary* and *Queen Elizabeth.*

The second all-action period was in 1944 when the prefabricated oil-line Pluto was installed to pump oil all the way from the Isle of Wight, and so many Allied supply ships came in that for a year Cherbourg carried more traffic than New York.

Between times, even the French seemed to have forgotten Cherbourg's existence. Only yachtsmen, many British, seemed to care. Now much of the ornate transatlantic terminal has been demolished, the main traffic is in car ferries from Britain, and the importance of Cherbourg to France is as a yard for building and operating submarines. It has summer boats to Guernsey in the British Channel Isles.

Cherbourg seems at last to be accepting its lesser role and is becoming a pleasant, modern town, with good specialist shops (for such items as cheese) and an excellent fish market. Like all ports with ferries from Britain, it has a hypermarket, but shopping around the streets is more fun and much more rewarding. If you are buying wine, for instance, Caves du Roy in rue Tour Carrée lets you taste before you buy. Parking is still hellish in Cherbourg, so it pays to park on the quai d'Entrepôt across the harbour basin and walk over the bridge.

Place Général de Gaulle has been rebuilt. You can wander round several shopping precincts or sit outside a café among spraying fountains watching people on Monday, Wednesday, Friday and Saturday. There is a very good market here on Tuesday, Thursday and Saturday morning for butter, cheese, vegetables, fruit and clothes.

Streets on one side of the square are for pedestrians only

and have a number of expensive boutiques and shoe shops. Streets beyond are good for shops selling cooked meats, bread and cakes. Grand'Rue is best for food. Near the fish market is a new shopping area in rue au Blé, with many boutiques selling clothes with such labels as Yves St Laurent, Cardin and Lapidus and touristy antique and gift shops.

More than three hundred years ago Vauban, the great military engineer, fortified Cherbourg and called it 'Tomorrow's Channel Inn'. But work on the breakwater to make it into a port was not begun for nearly a century and it was another seventy-seven years before cones, stuffed with rubble and mortar and sunk to make a base, accumulated sufficient strength to be used. Cherbourg had missed the boat. The port was not opened until 1853. The naval base planned by Napoleon I was opened by Napoleon III. The first transatlantic ship berthed there in 1869. But the new big liners could not get in until a deep-water channel was dredged in 1933.

When the Germans were driven out by the Americans on 27 June 1944, they sank blockships and mines in the harbour, but Royal Navy frogmen (called literally *hommes-grenouilles* by the French) cleared it in record time so that the port could take over from the temporary Mulberry Harbour at Arromanches and the Pluto oil line could start operating by 12 August 1944.

Cherbourg has two interesting museums. The War and Liberation Museum in Fort du Roule (shut Tuesday in winter) includes maps showing the progress of the war from D-Day 6 June 1944 until German capitulation 7 May, 1945. Musée Thomas-Henry, place République (Beaux-Arts museum) has not many pictures but has some high-quality works, including two 18th-century Italian masterpieces (a Pietà believed to be by Filippino Lippi) and Fra Angelico's *Conversion of St Augustin*, also thirty paintings and drawings of rural life in this area by Jean-François Millet, born in 1814 in nearby Gruchy, where his house still stands. He was the son of a peasant and few have painted country scenes so authentically. Later he lived in Jersey.

A road winds up to the fort on top of Roule Hill (112 metres high) from where there are fine views over town and harbour. The Germans made their last stand here.

Emmanuel Liais park is famous for tropical plants.

The northern coastline around Cherbourg is very rugged and spectacular (see introduction).

TOURIST INFORMATION quai Alexandre III
(33.43.52.02)
MARKETS Fish market daily, except Sunday. Mixed market in place Gén. de Gaulle Tuesday, Thursday, Saturday mornings

HOTELS

Frankly, there are so many nice smaller places within a short drive that I would not stay overnight in Cherbourg.
Louvre, 2 rue Henri-Dunant (33.53.02.28): no restaurant; rooms modernised, triple-glazed against traffic noise. ROOMS B–E. Shut mid-December–1 January.

RESTAURANTS

Chez Pain (Le Plouc), 59 rue au Blé (33.53.67.64): the best we have found so far among a rather poor selection of eating places. Very personally run by the Pains, with Jacky Pain doing the cooking (traditional with some personal touches). Good value menu. MEALS C–G. Shut Saturday lunch, Sunday.
Grandgousier, 21 rue l'Abbaye (33.53.19.43): bistro style; reliable; some very good dishes. MEALS C. Shut Saturday lunch; 20–31 March, 18 August–4 September.

At Urville–Nacqueville (11km from Cherbourg)
Manoir de Dur Ecu (33.03.45.43): lovely Norman manor now a farm-restaurant, with local products – St Vaast oysters, lamb. Cheap menus superb value. MEALS A–F. Shut Sunday evening, Monday.

Mont-St-Michel

[MANCHE, MAP 7, page 227]

Mont-St-Michel, *'Le Premier Site de France'*, 'the wonder of the Western world', may have been slightly oversold by tourist propagandists, but it *is* wonderful and, like Rocamadour, you remember your first sight of it for the rest of your life. Not surprising, for it was the Archangel Michael himself who, in the 8th century, told the Bishop of Avranches (St Aubert) that he wanted a chapel built on the mound – and tapped the cleric's head with his fingers to stress the point. It was a feat of engineering in those days to have built a great church on the summit of an eighty-metre granite peak rising out of the sea. In sunshine it stands like a mirage in a desert of sand. In sea-mist it looks like a fairy castle in the clouds. The outgoing tide leaves miles of mud and sand – quicksand, some of it, through which the monks of the abbey knew their way and their enemies could die. The English never took the abbey in the Hundred Years War. But they surrounded it, and when pilgrims came, they charged them a toll. Even then, hoteliers and souvenir salesmen made a good thing out of this holy mound, selling emblems bearing the head of St Michael and lead caskets of sand from the beach. The tides came in at a rate of fifty metres a minute over fifteen km. Many pilgrims were drowned or sunk in quicksands. It was known as St Michael's in Peril of the Sea. The present causeway was not built until 1874.

Centuries ago the whole bay was a huge forest, stretching to the Channel Isles. On the mound where St Michael's stands, Druids worshipped the sun. Then Romans built a temple to Jupiter, and later Christian hermits built a chapel. Then the great tides of the early 8th century cut off the Channel Isles

Mont-St-Michel

from the mainland, turning the mound into an island at high tide. People fled there from Viking marauders and a colony grew below the mount.

After St Aubert built St Michael's Chapel it became such an important place of pilgrimage that in 966 Richard, Duke of Normandy, replaced it with a Benedictine Abbey, which grew rich with endowments. They came not only from Normandy but from Brittany too, which used to lay claim to the abbey, which is inside Normandy by the width of a river, and from England, Edward the Confessor gave the priory of St Michael's Mount, off Penzance in Cornwall, to Mont-St-Michel. William the Conqueror enriched it with gifts, too. Troops of the French King Philippe-Auguste, besieging it in 1203, set fire to the abbey when storming it. So he paid for the building of the great Gothic fortress abbey you can see today. It was called *La Merveille* (the Marvel), and here the monks entertained kings and the rich and important. The nave was twice its present length of 70 metres.

In 1780 the Romanesque façade was replaced by a Classical façade and half the nave knocked down. But this did clear the way for the terrace (*plate-forme de l'Ouest*) from which you now have magnificent views over Mont-St-Michel bay. The Guests' Hall, the majestic Knights' Hall and the cloisters, which seem to be suspended half way to heaven, are superb.

The abbey's heyday was in the reign of Louis XIV when it was enlarged and made more beautiful. Decline came with commendatory abbots – men, not always churchmen, given abbeys by kings as a sinecure. They could live off an abbey's funds without even visiting it. Discipline slackened among the monks. After the French Revolution, when the monks were driven out, Napoleon I turned the abbey into a prison. Prisoners made straw hats in the church. Restoration began in 1874 when the abbey was declared a national monument. Not until 1966 (a thousand years after the Benedictine abbey was built) did Benedictine monks hold services in the church again.

You need to be reasonably fit to climb the ninety steps leading to the terrace – or in summer to push your way uphill through thousands of tourists, past souvenir shops, crêperies and restaurants, to reach the abbey. Only six thousand people are allowed inside at a time, so you might have to wait.

Apart from the abbey itself, you can visit the 13th to 15th-century ramparts, with views across the bay, the abbey gardens, the Historical Museum (open every day, early June–mid October; weekdays only, end March–end May) with waxworks of the abbey's history and a collection of 25,000 clock balance cocks (part of old clock mechanisms), and Musée de la Mer (mostly about local maritime matters but including two hundred old boat models – shut in January).

Walking round the outside of the Mount takes thirty to forty minutes but do check times of tides before starting.

TOURIST INFORMATION Corps de Guard de Bourgeois
at Mount entrance (33.60.14.30 or 33.60.00.35)
FÊTES July – beach pilgrimage when processions walk
across the sands. September – St Michael's Autumn
Festival and Fair (splendid but very crowded). May – St
Michael's Spring Fair. July–August – Festival of Music

HOTELS WITH RESTAURANTS

Mère Poulard (33.60.14.01): part of the Mount's history. Annette Poulard's omelettes were world renowned. People visited her first to watch her making and cooking them. Since she died in 1931, her restaurant has varied from very good to mediocre. Now it is good again with Jean-Claude Pierpaoli running it and Jean-Luc Whal not only cooking omelettes but the famous local *pré-salé* lamb from the salt-marshes, salmon, sole, prawns, lobster and superb oysters. Up rickety stairs are bedrooms with sea-views. ROOMS F–G. MEALS D–G. Shut mid-November–mid-February.

Terrasses Poulard (33.60.14.09): hotel delightfully converted from historic house; rooms small but charming, with views over sea or town. Restaurant large, touristy, with straightforward cooking, good value. 'Mediaeval' banquets. ROOMS E–G. MEALS A–E. Half-board only high season.

La Digue, 2km on D976 (33.60.14.02): modern, comfortable; view of bay and Mount from restaurant. Good value meals. ROOMS D–E. MEALS A–E. Hotel shut mid-November–mid-February. Restaurant shut 20 October–20 March.

Du Guesclin (33.60.14.10): long-popular simple Logis de France, run by M. Nicolle, pioneer of Logis de France organisation. Meals good value. ROOMS A–D. MEALS A-F. Shut mid-October–Easter; Wednesday low-season.

D-Day Beaches

[MAP 2, *below*]

The Allied landings in Normandy on 6 June 1944, which began the liberation of France and Europe are fading from vivid memory into history. As my generation becomes older and thinner on the ground, memories of fear and anguish, heroism and sorrow are material for films and TV programmes, and the story is told in museums and on memorials which have sprung up along the beaches and in the towns of Normandy. It has taken modern techniques of science to tell the story from 1918 to the present in the biggest museum of all at Caen – '*Une Musée pour la Paix*' set up as a Memorial to the Battle of Normandy. And that did not open until 1988.

This is no place to go into details of military operations, of successes and mistakes, of horrors and heroism. Let us look at the beaches where the Allies landed and the museums which can be visited.

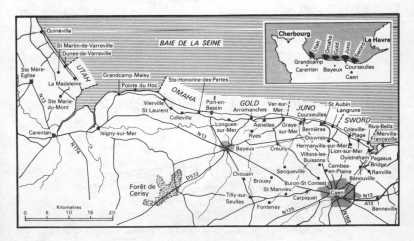

2   *The D-Day Beaches*

BÉNOUVILLE

The first landing of D-Day was not on a beach and was not on D-Day itself (6 June). After darkness on 5 June British Airborne units – gliders and parachutists – landed at the villages of Bénouville and Ranville to take the bridge crossing the canal and a bridge over the river Orne. At 11.45 p.m. Captain John Howard and parachutists of the Oxford and Buckinghamshire Regiment (5th Parachute Brigade) took the canal bridge, the town hall and the canal-side *auberge* – 'the first house to be freed in France'. They held them well into the next day when Lord Lovat's No. 6 Commando arrived, led by a Scottish piper and '2½ minutes late on schedule', as the canal-side memorial points out – hardly a court-martial offence considering they had been first to land on Sword Beach at dawn and had fought their way through strong German units, including tanks. The canal bridge has been named Pegasus Bridge after the symbol of the Airborne Forces. The old inn has re-opened. Next door is a very interesting museum with pictures, plans, weapons, uniforms (open daily 22 March–15 October). Ranville nearby was taken by an airborne unit of the Lancashire Fusiliers.

SWORD BEACH
[Ouistreham Riva-Bella west to Langrune]

British and French Commandos landed first, including the 4th Commando under Commandant Philippe Kiefer and the 6th Commando under Lord Lovat, and took the strongpoints at Riva-Bella, Coleville-Plage, Lion-sur-Mer and St Aubin. Then the British 3rd Infantry Brigade landed with two tank brigades and the 51st Highland Division which had fought much of the rearguard action in the Dunkirk evacuation in 1940. (They had written '51st Division – we're back' on their tanks.) The objective was to take Caen. General Montgomery (Commander-in-Chief of the Land Forces under Supreme Allied Commander General Eisenhower) realised that Caen was the hinge of the whole landing and that this was the toughest front, especially as the beaches were exposed to the German long-range guns at Le Havre. Several villages were taken quickly but the German 21st Panzer Division launched a fierce counter-attack and although a deep bridgehead was established, Caen was not freed until mid-July – what was left of it.

MUSEUMS AND MONUMENTS
Commemorative monuments at Bénouville and Ouistreham. War Museums at Riva-Bella (Museum No. 4 Commando, place Alfred Thomas, showing liberation of the seaside resort by Anglo-French Commandos – open each day 1 June–15 September; weekends 1 March–1 May). Bénouville (6th Airborne Division Museum – open daily 22 March–15 October). Merville–Franceville (Merville Battery – taken by British Airborne troops at dawn on D-Day; small museum – open June, July, August except Tuesdays). Caen (Memorial for the Battle of Normandy Museum dedicated to Peace, open daily except Monday in winter).

CEMETERIES
British Cemeteries at Banneville, Douvres; Hermanville-sur-Mer and Ranville.

JUNO BEACH
[St Aubin to Grave-sur-Mer]

The Canadian 3rd Infantry Division (including British units) landed from 7 a.m. onwards at Bernières and Courseulles, reaching Creully by 5 p.m. Strong German defence of two radar stations held them up and one objective, Carpiquet, was not reached, so liaison with the 3rd British Division was not made.

MUSEUMS AND MONUMENTS
Commemorative monument at Bernières. Other monuments at Courseulles, St Aubin, Villons-les-Buissons and Buron-St Contest.

CEMETERIES
Bény-sur-Mer (Canadian), Cambes-en-Plaine (British).

GOLD BEACH
(Ver-sur-Mer to Port-en-Bessin]

The success of the landings depended totally on the capture of
Arromanches so that the artificial Mulberry Harbour could be
set up. The Germans had assumed that the Allies must capture a
major port immediately to supply their forces. Their Intelli-
gence seemed totally unaware of the existence of the prefabricated harbour made in pieces in many different parts of
Britain, to be towed across to a landing beach, just as they were
equally unaware of the undersea Pluto oil pipe bringing oil from
the Isle of Wight to Cherbourg. There were two Mulberries –
one at Arromanches for the British, one on Omaha Beach for
the Americans (this one broke up on 19 June in the worst storm
for forty years). 1,416 Phoenix caisons were laid made of
600,000 tons of concrete, plus 33 jetties and floating 'roads' for
landing vehicles 16km long. All this had been towed across
the Channel at 6km per hour. Arromanches Mulberry enabled
9000 tons of materials to be landed each day until the end of
August, when Cherbourg and Antwerp were operating again as
ports.

The British 50th Northumbrian Division landed at 7.25 a.m.
on D-Day at Ver-sur-Mer and Asnelles and by a brilliant flanking movement had taken Arromanches beach by the afternoon. The Royal Engineers did a brilliant job of clearing
anti-invasion devices. Meanwhile No. 47 Royal Marines Commando fought their way 20km through German defences to
take Port-en-Bessin by the following evening (7 June) and by 9
June had linked up with the Americans landing on Omaha
Beach. By 12 June, at Carentan, the link was completed with US
troops from Utah Beach and the beach-head was solid and safe.
Inland, beautiful Bayeux was liberated so fast by the Northumberlands that it was hardly damaged – the first town in France to
be liberated. One reason for the quick success was that the main

German defence battery near Longues-sur-Mer with guns with a 20km range was knocked out by the British cruiser, *Ajax*, and the French cruisers *Montcalm* and *Georges-Leygues*. But inland later German counter-attacks were so fierce that the little village of Tilly-sur-Seulles was taken and retaken 23 times between 7–30 June.

MUSEUMS AND MONUMENTS

MONUMENTS Bayeux – Liberation Memorial; Port-en-Bessin. MUSEUMS Arromanches – Invasion Museum (Musée Débarquement) on beach opposite remains of Mulberry Harbour is best of the landing museums, with models, plans, arms, equipment and Royal Navy films of the landing (open daily except 25 December). Bayeux – 'Memorial 1944', boul. Fabian-Ware tracing fighting from 7 June to 22 August – open daily 1 March–30 October, weekends January, February). Tilly-sur-Seulles (Museum of the Battle for Tilly – open daily in June, July, August; weekends September).

CEMETERIES

British cemeteries at Bayeux, Brouay, Chouain, Fontenay, Ryes, St Manvieu, Secqueville, Tilly.

OMAHA BEACH
[Ste-Honorine-des-Pertes to Grandcamp Maisy]

US landing on this narrow beach with cliffs was the most costly landing operation. At 4.30 a.m. the 225 Rangers climbed the Pointe du Hoc brilliantly but were pinned down by German forces until 8 June. Seas were rough and not enough allowance had been made for the strong coastal current, so when the first wave of troops of the 1st US Infantry Division started to land at 6.30 a.m. their landing craft drifted off-course and there were heavy casualties. German artillery hit the second wave, the beach had not been cleared of anti-invasion devices and the tide was rising. Heavy armour could not move on shingle. Then two destroyers moved inshore to shell the German artillery and small assault groups gained the coast road by the evening, enabling motorised units to gain the plateau.

MUSEUMS AND MONUMENTS

COMMEMORATIVE MONUMENTS at St Laurent-sur-Mer, Isigny-sur-Mer, Pointe du Hoc.
MUSEUMS at Vierville (Omaha Exhibition – open daily April–September).

CEMETERY

Colleville-St Laurent (US).

UTAH BEACH
[Carentan to Quineville]

US Airborne troops of the 101st and 82nd Divisions were dropped before the landing in an arc south of Ste-Mère-Église. Though rough seas meant that the 4th US Infantry Division started to land at La Madeleine and the Dunes-de-Varreville two miles south of where they intended, and despite heavy German gunfire, defences were weak and by midday the beach was cleared. A US detachment pushed inland to Chef-du-Pont and linked up with the 82nd Airborne paras. Three weeks later the Cotentin Peninsula was cleared of German troops and, most importantly, the port of Cherbourg had been freed.

MUSEUMS AND MEMORIALS

COMMEMORATIVE MONUMENTS at La Madeleine, Carentan, Ste-Mère-Église and St-Martin-de-Varreville (US); Dunes-de-Varreville (French – commemorating the landing on 1 August) of General Leclerc's famous Free French Armoured Division). Ste-Marie-du-Mont (Danish – to the eight hundred Danish sailors who took part).
MUSEUM Cherbourg (Liberation Museum at Fort du Roule – open daily except Tuesday low-season), Ste-Marie-du-Mont (Utah Beach Museum – open early April–end October). Ste-

Mère-Église (US Airborne Museum – open daily morning and afternoon except mid-November, when weekends only).

CEMETERY

Marigny (US).

END OF THE BATTLE

With the British and Canadians engaging 5½ of the 6 German Panzer Divisions in Normandy while the Americans swept through to the south of them (by Montgomery's directive in early July), the battle for Normandy was over by 21 August. The Germans had lost 640,000 men, killed, wounded or taken prisoner. The Allies lost 210,000, of whom 37,000 were killed.

PLACES

ACQUIGNY
[EURE]

A hamlet in an attractive stretch of the Eure valley where the Eure meets the river Iton (on D71 5km S of Louviers). 16th-century Renaissance château and park look attractive from Eure bridge.

RESTAURANT
Hostellerie, 32.50.20.05: MEALS A. Shut 4–24 August; 15–28 February; Sunday evening, Monday

AGON
[MANCHE – *See* Coutainville page 117]

L'AIGLE
[ORNE]

Called the 'pins and needles capital' for its long-established steel industry. On the Risle river, busy. St Martin's Church is an attractive muddle of contrasting styles with 12th-century tower of iron with spires, elaborately sculptured 15th-century Flamboyant-Gothic square tower. Some 16th-century windows harmonise with superb modern glass by Max Ingrand. The 17th-century château was designed by Jules Hardouin-Mansart, Louis XIV's chief architect for Versailles, for the Marquis de l'Aigle. Used in the French Revolution as a Tribunal for trying and sentencing aristocrats, it was heavily bombed in 1944, repaired, and is now the town hall. In an outbuilding is a museum of the Battle of Normandy with wax figures of de Gaulle, Général Leclerc, Churchill, Roosevelt and Stalin with records of their voices. (Shut Monday in winter.) Information 1 place F.de Beina (33.24.12.40) in season.

MARKET Tuesdays (large)

HOTEL

Dauphin, place de la Halle (33.24.43.12): 12th-century Relais with refitted bedrooms and big Anglo-Norman style dining room. Excellent cooking of Norman dishes with individual touches. Not cheap. Huge choice of Calvados. ROOMS E–F. MEALS C–G.

RESTAURANT

Auberge Saint-Michel, at St Michel-Tuboeuf, 3½km E on N26 (33.24.20.12): Norman country inn. MEALS B–D. Shut Wednesday evening, Thursday; February.

ALENÇON
[ORNE]

A market town on the Sarthe river whose old buildings and narrow streets mostly survived the 1944 fighting, it is an excellent exploring centre, surrounded by delightful country of the Perche and on the edge of the Normandy-Maine National Park. Écouves Forest southward is a lovely refuge in every season – a forest of mixed trees with deer and wild boar, paths for walking, avenues for driving (*see* Écouves Forest page 128). To the southeast is the Perseigne Forest, another attractive mixed forest of oak, beech and fir and to the south-west the Mancelles Alpes – an exaggerated name for a most pleasant, quiet region of steep, heather-covered granite hills enfolding the Sarthe valley. Since the 17th century Alençon has been famous for 'Point d'Alençon' lace, a craft introduced by Colbert, the astute chief minister of Louis XIV. He resented ladies of fashion wasting precious currency on lace from Venice. Alas, you can no longer watch the lace being made. Few women can be enticed into this hard, intricate and sight-destroying work. A piece 3 cm square can take sixteen hours and eye-strain is so bad that makers can only work three hours a day. No wonder that the few pieces still made by hand cost a small fortune. You can see the work of yesteryear in the Lace Museum (Musée de la Dentelle – open all weekdays 15 May–15 September; closed Monday rest of year). You can see a film of the history and technique of lace-making and some exquisite pieces of lace, some so delicate you should view them through a magnifying glass. The veil worn by Marie-Antoinette is outstandingly beautiful. Another lace collection is in the Musée des Beaux-Arts, now moved to an old Jesuit College from the town hall. The display shows the development of the craft and a tour of the other main lace-making centres of the past – Venice, Flanders (Brussels), England (Nottingham) and France (Chantilly, Le Puy, Argentan, Bayeux).

In the same museum is a collection to warm the hearts of amateurs of French painting. There are fine works here from the 17th to 20th centuries of artists less known to most of us, including paintings taken from churches and abbeys in the Revolution. Outstanding of these are Jouvenet's *Marriage of the Virgin* and Philippe de Champaigne's *Assumption*. Typical coastal scenes by Boudin and a landscape by Courbet are excellent, and the drawings include works of Watteau and Bourdon. One of the finest paintings is *Christ Carrying the Cross* by the Spaniard José Ribera. (Shut Monday.)

There are still fine old houses in Alençon, many with window boxes, charming little lanes, and a beautiful Flamboyant Cathedral Notre Dame. It was finished in 1444 but the tower, transept and chancel were reconstructed in the 18th century. The unusual Flamboyant three-sided porch with gables, bell towers and spires took from 1490 to 1506 to build. The stained glass from 1530 in the nave is exceptional.

You can see two towers of the old Duke of Alençon's castle from place Foch. They are from the 14th and 15th centuries. The rest has been much restored. Here the brilliant Marguerite of Angoulême, sister of Francois I, widow of the Duc d' Angoulême, grandmother of the great Henri IV of France, held court with distinguished poets and writers. She herself was a poet and writer of much ability. In 1940 the Gestapo took the castle over as a prison and many French patriots and Resistance fighters were tortured or killed within its walls. It is still a prison today.

Up a double staircase opposite the Préfecture (a fine 17th-century building) is the Chapel of Ste Thérèse of Lisieux, next to the house in which she was born in 1873 as Thérèse Martin. A vast basilica was built to her at Lisieux (see page 160).

The tourist office is in a fine 15th-century house with quiet garden – Maison d'Ozé.

In the Écouves forest, Général Leclerc's Free French Tank Division defeated a German Panzer Division and liberated Alençon, the first French town to be liberated after D-Day by French forces.

TOURIST INFORMATION 1 Maison d'Ozé,
place Lamagdelaine (33.26.11.36)
MARKETS Friday, Sunday
FESTIVALS September – music

HOTELS

Chapeau Rouge, 1 boul. Duchamp (33.26.20.23): pretty white house on busy road but recently soundproofed. No restaurant. ROOMS B–E.

RESTAURANTS

Petit Vatel, 72 place Cdt. Demeulles (33.26.23.78): Balzac's oft-mentioned gourmands of Alençon would look no further than Michel Lerat's restaurant. A traditional Norman chef who has great respect for fresh seasonal ingredients from the market (superb salmon in cider), he experiments, too, with dishes like *St Pierre* (John Dory) with peaches and mussels in spinach. Excellent vegetables. MEALS C–F. Shut 15–31 August, part February; Wednesday, Sunday evening.

ALLOUVILLE-BELLEFOSSE
[SEINE-MARITIME]

A village of fewer than a thousand people in the Pays de Caux is famous all over France for its oak tree – thirteen centuries old – alongside the church. Its trunk and biggest branches are supported. The trunk is ten metres round. In 1669 the curé built two superimposed chapels into hollows of the trunk, reached by stairs around the trunk. Before the Revolution it had two neighbours – an oak and a fir, said to have been as big. The Revolutionaries burned them but saved the big oak as a 'Temple of Reason'. Screen writer Alphonse Boudard used it as the 'hero' of a film story in 1980.

1½km from the village is an interesting Musée de la Nature set up in 1980 showing the animals and plants of Normandy, and the dangers of pollution (shut Tuesdays in winter). It has, too, a hospital for sick and wounded animals and birds, many wounded by hunters or covered in oil. An international folklore festival is held at Whitsun.

ALMENÊCHES
[ORNE]

Renaissance church was once part of Benedictine abbey. Nice horse country 6km SW of the Haras du Pin stud (page 178) near Château d'O (page 173).

LES ANDELYS
[EURE]

From a clifftop at Gaillard Castle you have long views over sheltered Grand Andely and the riverside village of Petit Andely to surrounding country far across the river Seine. The castle was built here in 1196 for that reason by Richard Coeur de Lion,

Plantagenet King of England, Duke of Normandy and Count of Anjou. He wanted to bar the route to Rouen from the French. While Richard lived, Philippe-Auguste of France dared not attack it. But when the weaker King John reigned, Philippe took it in a remarkable assault in which the French got in through the latrines, let down the drawbridge and swarmed in. Rouen fell to France in three months and the French annexed Normandy. A Scottish king, David Bruce, lived here when he fled to France in 1334. Before that two French queens, Blanche, wife of 'Charles IV, and Marguerite, wife of Louis X were imprisoned in the castle for sleeping with boy-friends. Marguerite was strangled there with her own hair because the king wanted to marry again. You can reach the castle by driving to the car park, from which there is a fine view of the castle, the Seine and the town. The last climb, fairly stiff, must be done on foot. Much of Grand Andely was destroyed in June 1940 but the 16th-century church survives, with a fine organ and beautiful stained glass, from 14th century to modern windows by Gaudin. Grand Andely gets very crowded in summer.

Petit Andely, undamaged in the war, has a new marina where Seine fishermen used to keep their boats, a mid-river island with the abandoned mansion of a millionaire and the 18th-century Chaîne d'Or coaching inn. It is named after the chain which locals used to dangle across the river to stop Seine barges and boats until they had paid a toll – so lucrative that it was called 'the golden chain'.

TOURIST INFORMATION 1 rue Philippe-Auguste,
15 March–15 November (32.54.41.93)
MARKET Monday

HOTELS

Chaîne d'Or, place St Sauveur, Petit Andely (32.54.00.31): overlooking Seine. Known for fine Norman cooking and sauces (duck in apples, cream and calvados; *sauce armoricaine* with salmon terrine). Recently started to turn modern with inevitable magret of duck and pigeon half-raw, warm (*tiède*) salads, vegetable mousselines, but very good cooking and old French inn atmosphere. Bedrooms vary from small to huge. ROOMS B–E.

MEALS D–G. Shut 2 January–2 February; Sunday evening, Monday low season.

Normandie, 1 rue Grande, Petit Andely (32.54.10.52): very old inn overlooking Seine. Some good Norman dishes. ROOMS A–D. MEALS B–E. Shut December; Wednesday evening, Thursday.

APPEVILLE-ANNEBAULT
[EURE]

Hamlet in the Risle river valley where the D130 follows the river and the Montfort forest. Large 14th-century church, partly rebuilt in 16th century, when an Admiral had the idea of making the river navigable and this the main port. It contains a collection of unusual 'Brothers of Charity' staffs.

ARGENTAN
[ORNE]

Considering how badly damaged it was in 1944, Argentan has been reborn as a pleasant little town with a nice atmosphere. Happily, both the town's churches, St Germain, with a lantern tower and impressive Flamboyant porch, and St Martin, Gothic-Renaissance with an octagonal tower, escaped enough to be repaired.

In the Benedictine Abbey nuns still make the Argentan lace created here – *La Point d'Argentan* – different from *Point d'Alençon*. You can see specimens (afternoons except Sundays). The design was rediscovered in 1874 by accident. In the old market place Henry II of England uttered the fateful phrase in 1170, 'Will no-one rid me of this turbulent priest?' and over-zealous knights went to Canterbury and murdered Thomas à Becket on the steps of the cathedral.

Traditionally Argentan was a market town for cattle of the plateau. Birthplace of the painter, Fernand Léger (1881–1955), who was inspired by Cézanne and early Cubism, but created a

formal style which he used to portray modern urban and technological advances.

The 1944 destruction came when on 19 August British and
Canadian and Polish Forces advancing from the north-west
joined American and French Forces coming from the south in a
pincer in the valley of the Dives north-east of Argentan and
destroyed the retreating German 7th Army, effectively ending
the Battle of Normandy.

TOURIST INFORMATION 1 place du Marché
(33.67.12.48)
MARKET Tuesday

HOTELS

La Renaissance, 20 ave 2e. Division Blindée (33.36.14.20): Michel
Moulin, former chef to the Duke of Windsor and Rothschilds,
here since 1969, is an individualist with his own delicious recipes
and his own smokery (including salmon). Charming dining
room. ROOMS B–E. MEALS B–F. Shut 15 September–15
October; Sunday low season.

France, 8 boul. Carnot (33.67.03.65): renovated; classic cooking,
good value meals. ROOMS C–E. MEALS A–E. Shut Sunday evenings. Restaurant shut 1–10 September, mid-February–mid-
March.

ARGUEIL
[SEINE-MARITIME]

Delightful village 9km S of Forges-les-Eaux; 16th-century
church with very tall, proud spire and 17th-century château,
lovely countryside. Old farms amid orchards down narrow
lanes.

ARQUES-LA-BATAILLE
[SEINE-MARITIME]

A little industrial town 7km SE of Dieppe, it was named for the great victory by Henri IV in 1589. With 7000 men and all the artillery he could muster he beat 30,000 troops of the extremist Catholic League (*see* Dieppe page 23). The imposing ruins of the castle still stand on a rock inside its old ramparts, from which there are fine views. Bombardment in World War Two caused much of the destruction. Notre Dame Church with twin turrets and pierced buttresses was rebuilt around 1515.

The state-owned beech forest east of Arques is bounded by the Béthune and Eaule rivers which meet here to form the river Arques. Routes through it are narrow in places. Martin-Église, village on the edge towards Dieppe, is still known for trout.

RESTAURANT WITH ROOMS
Hostellerie Manoir d'Archelles, on D1 (35.85.50.16): lovely small manor house; varying reports on food lately, mostly favourable. ROOMS C–D. MEALS A–F. Shut 1–14 August; Sunday evening; Monday.
Clos Normand, at Martin-Église (*see* Dieppe page 23).

ARROMANCHES-LES-BAINS
[CALVADOS]

The modest little family seaside resort became overnight one of the greatest battlegrounds in history as the British landed on 6 June 1944 and then set up the incredible Mulberry Harbour (*see* D-Day page 60). The Invasion Museum on the promenade, showing photographs, models and a Royal Navy film of the landing, explains what happened during that historic week (open every day except 25 December). And from an observation post just east of the town you can see through telescopes the remains of the concrete and steel jetties which were towed from England. Visitors to the museum almost swamp the resort in

summer and much of the old promenade is a huge car park. But
French families still take to the beach, and out of season
Arromanches reverts to its old seaside role; then there's time for
a chat in the shops, restaurants and cafés, and it is a pleasant
spot. Asnelles, at east end of Mulberry Harbour, has a rebuilt
promenade with views of Arromanches and cliffs.

TOURIST INFORMATION 1 place du Musée (31.22.36.45
– high-season)

HOTEL

Marine, quai Canada (31.22.34.19): cheap, simple hotel – right
on beach. Friendly, Norman regional cooking, good shellfish.
ROOMS D–E. MEALS A–D. Shut 15 November–1 March.

ASSY
[CALVADOS]

North 12km from Falaise to Soumont, then 3km NE is Château
d'Assy (1788), a perfect classical château, approached by a magnificent avenue. Wonderfully elegant Corinthian columns.

AUBIGNY
[CALVADOS]

3km N of Falaise, hamlet with a fine Louis XIII castle and even
older buildings around it.

AUMALE
[SEINE-MARITIME]

Dairy centre on the river Bresle, Aumale suffered badly in the
Nazi advance in 1940. One of the Counts of Aumale was

brother-in-law of William the Conqueror and fought at Hastings in 1066. His English descendants became the Albemarle family. Fighting the Spaniards, who held the Netherlands, Henri IV was wounded and actually lost a battle here in 1592 – a rare occurrence. The recently restored church of St Pierre and St Paul is Gothic with Renaissance features and 16th-century glass.

RESTAURANTS WITH ROOMS

Dauphin, 27 rue St Lazare (35.93.41.92): classic cooking, cheap menus excellent value. ROOMS C. MEALS B–G. Shut end June, 20 December–mid January; Sunday; Saturday evening except mid-summer.

Mouton Gras, 2 rue Verdun (35.93.41.32): in a fine 17th century Norman house with a lovely interior; good cooking, cheap. MEALS A–C. Shut mid-August–mid-September; Monday evening, Tuesday.

AUNAY-SUR-ODON
[CALVADOS]

Little town NW of Thury Harcourt totally smashed in three days in June 1944 was almost miraculously and beautifully replanned and rebuilt between November 1947 and August 1950. It is a lesson in subtle harmony. The local deep creamy and brown limestone is used for buildings capped by the blue-grey slate roofs, alongside colourful flower beds. The vast new church is a symbol of faith in the future.

TOURIST INFORMATION pl. Hotel de Ville (31.77.60.32)

RESTAURANT WITH ROOMS

St-Michel, rue Caen (31.77.63.16): Logis de France. ROOMS B–C. MEALS A–E. Shut mid–end November, mid-end January; Sunday evening, Monday out of season.

AUTHEUIL
[ORNE]

Hamlet NE of Mortagne-au-Perche just off N12 on edge of the beautiful Perche forest of oaks, beeches and pines. Attractive walks and drives. Interesting pure Romanesque church.

AVRANCHES
[MANCHE]

Avranches is a busy, likeable town above the Sée estuary, looking across the bay to Mont-St-Michel. Explore on foot, for it's a maze of little alleys, and crannies with old buildings. In Jardin des Plantes, the botanical gardens, is a terrace with a wonderful panorama of the bay, particularly magnificent by moonlight. The gardens, once part of a Capuchin monastery, have a waterfall and some fine trees – illuminated at night.

The Avranchin Museum in the former bishop's palace has 8th–15th century manuscripts, mostly from Mont-St-Michel Abbey (open Easter–30 September except Tuesdays).

Where the cathedral stood until 1794 you can see the stone (*La Plateforme*) on which Henry II of England knelt barefooted and dressed only in a shirt to receive absolution after his foolhardy knights had murdered Thomas à Becket at Canterbury.

Place Patton is American territory. Soil and trees were brought from different states of the US. From this spot on 1 August 1944 General George 'Blood and Guts' Patton and his newly formed 3rd Army of the US Forces launched their first attack against the Germans which took them across Europe. The Patton memorial has an inscription with more than a little of Patton's own theatrical style: 'Making the Avranches breakthrough in the roar of its tanks while marching towards victory and the liberation of France, the glorious American Army of General Patton passed over this cross-road.'

In Avranches in 1639 the peasants and saltworkers under Jean Quetil (Jean Nu-Pieds – John Barefoot) started an unsuccessful revolt which nevertheless had repercussions until the French Revolution. At Val St Père, 5km S is a 1944 war museum. The ground floor is devoted to the Germans, the first floor to the Allies. From the airfield nearby air trips fly over Mont-St-Michel – a superb way to see the abbey (April–mid-September – tel: 33.58.02.91). A footpath 228km long (Sentier Tour du Cotentin – GR 223) goes right round the coast to St Vaast and Barfleur on the north-east tip of the peninsula.

TOURIST INFORMATION Tourist Office, rue Gén. de Gaulle (33.58.00.22)
MARKET Saturday

HOTELS

Croix d'Or 83 rue Constitution (33.58.04.88): pretty Norman posting inn; authentic old décor. Comfortable bedrooms. Garden. Norman cooking with some modernisation. Try *dodine de canard* (boned, stuffed duck). Good fish. ROOMS B–F. MEALS B–G. Shut mid-November–mid-March.

Auberge St Michel, 7 place Patton (33.58.01.91): nice atmosphere. Renovated rooms. Garden. Meals good value, Norman dishes (*pré-salé* lamb; fish in cider). ROOMS B–D. MEALS A–E. Shut 15 November–31 March; Sunday evening, Monday 15 September–15 June.

BAGNOLES-DE-L'ORNE
[ORNE]

This dignified, elegant and quiet spa where once solemn, older French couples enjoyed discussing their ailments, has suddenly become crowded with holidaymakers and peace-destroying traffic in mid-summer. A quite lively centre for exploring the great beauties of the neighbouring Écouves Forest and the surrounding woods, hills, lush meadows and streams rich in trout; still an attractive place, almost smugly cleaned, brushed and painted, with grass trimmed and formal flower-beds weedless. Its white casino shines in the well-tended lake and the boutiques and cafés fill with well-heeled visitors.

The story of the spa's discovery is a repeat of many others. Hugues de Tesse, not wanting to kill his charger, Rapide, who was old and sick, let him loose in the forest. The horse returned frisky, with shining coat and bright eyes . . . So Hugues followed his hoof marks, found the spring and pools, bathed in them, and he became frisky, too. People would brave the wolves and muggers of the forest to reach the springs. Perhaps nude mixed bathing encouraged them. Now it is all formalised in a thermal establishment in an attractive park. The Great Spring water flows at 50000 litres an hour at 27°C, has few minerals and much radioactivity. It is used for circulation troubles, phlebitis, to prevent varicose veins and reduce obesity. It would do me no harm whatsoever.

The best view of Bagnoles is from Roc au Chien, a rocky promontory reached by steps, half-way to Tessé-la-Madeleine, now almost part of Bagnoles but less crowded. The château here, now the town hall, looks like a Renaissance manor but was built around 1850 by a rich lady.

TOURIST INFORMATION 1 place de la Gare, Bagnoles
(33.37.80.04)
FESTIVAL July in Bagnoles
MARKET Wednesday

HOTELS

Manoir du Lys, 3km on D335, D235 (33.37.80.69): delightful little manor with a delightful welcome and delicious cooking by Paul Quinton, patron-chef; in autumn he takes guests into the forest, teaches them to identify edible fungi, then shows how to cook them. Nice garden. Tennis. Charming bedrooms. ROOMS E–F. MEALS C–G. Open 15 March–31 October, weekends in November, December. Shut Sunday evening, Monday from 15 March–30 April.

Lutétia Hotel, Restaurant Reine Astrid, boul. Paul-Chalvet (33.37.94.77) 'grand' hotel in big garden; very comfortable; excellent cooking. ROOMS D–F. MEALS C–G. Shut early November–end March.

Grand Venent, 6 place République (33.37.86.79): old favourite; family run. Good value. Norman dishes. ROOMS C–E. MEALS A–E. Shut mid-October–31 March.

La Bruyère, at Michel-des-Andaines, 2km N on D908
(33.37.22.26): simple, old-style inn with garden in Andaine
forest. Known for local dishes (veal normande and tripe on
skewer cooked over open fire). ROOMS B–C. MEALS A–D. Shut
1 November–28 February.

BALLEROY
[CALVADOS]

20km SW Bayeux. A single, wide street of elegant houses, once a
great avenue, leads to the lovely grey-and-pink château. Beautifully proportioned, it has been called a 'miniature Versailles',
although it is less exuberant. Anyway, it predates Versailles. It
was built for Jean de Choisy by François Mansart between 1616
and 1636 and the marquises of Balleroy lived there for three
centuries. The formal gardens and terrace were designed by Le
Nôtre who designed Versailles' gardens. The interior decoration
is superb. The drawing room has a fine French-style painted
ceiling and both this and the dining room have portraits by
François Mignard (lesser known than brother Pierre) which
show famous Frenchmen in a different light from the usual
flattering portraits. Louis XIII, Condé, Mme de Montespan,
Louis XIV, his brother Philippe d' Orléans and his mother Anne
of Austria are among them.

The present owner is an American magazine-owner, Mal-
colm Forbes, also a world record-breaking balloonist. In an
outbuilding is a very interesting balloon museum, and an annual
international balloon rally is held in June in the castle grounds.
(All open March–September except Wednesday.) The parish
church, by Mansart, was originally the castle chapel.

HOTEL
Des Biards, 1 place du Marché (31.21.60.05): simple village inn
with bargain prices and good welcome. Good cider. ROOMS
A–B. MEALS A–C. Shut January, February; Monday.

BARENTIN
[SEINE-MARITIME]

As you enter this little industrial town 17km NW of Rouen you
see the Statue of Liberty! It was built for the French film *Le
Cerveau* (The Brain). The streets are a sort of open-air museum
of modern sculptors – Rodin, Bourdelle, Janniot, Gromaire.

BARFLEUR
[MANCHE]

This little port with a mere 720 people, beloved by yachtsmen
and families who like messing about in boats, once saw scenes
in the Middle Ages which changed history. In 1066 the town
sent the ship on which William the Bastard, Duke of Normandy,
embarked at Dives on his journey to become William the Conqueror, King of England. It was piloted by a Barfleur man. In
1120 the White Ship carrying the heir to Henry I of England,
William Atheling, from Barfleur to England, foundered in the
shallow waters and swift currents, drowning him and a hundred
young noblemen of his court. Only the butcher survived. This
time the Barfleur pilot was drunk. The prince might have got
away in a small boat if he had not insisted on going back to try to
rescue his natural sister, the Countess of Mortagne. Other
people swarmed onto his boat and sank it. Then in 1154, after
King Stephen of England's death, Henry II, his heir arrived in
Barfleur in mid-November to sail to England to claim the
throne. Winds were so strong that he could not sail until 8
December and was not crowned in Westminster Abbey until 19
December. And in 1194 Richard Coeur de Lion sailed from
Barfleur to be crowned King of England.

    Barfleur is a tiny, family holiday resort in summer. Its fishing
fleet has almost disappeared though local boats bring in mussels
cultivated nearby, and artists still paint the harbour and town. It
looks its best at high tide.

    Gatteville, 2½km NE, has a 12th-century seafarers' church,

rebuilt in the 17th century, but with its original belfry. Parts of
old wall paintings and a 15th-century altar were revealed during
repair work in 1956. The road which leads on to the lighthouse
at Pointe de Barfleur crosses windswept fields rich in wild
flowers from spring to autumn, with white spray rising from the
rocks below. The lighthouse is the tallest in France (71 metres).
From the top is a wonderful panorama of the coast, and as the
tide seeps in, an almost frightening sight of the granite rocks
sinking under the sea.

Westward at the hamlet of Tocqueville is the 15th to 18th
century château where Alexis de Tocqueville (1805–59) lived.
He wrote *Democracy in America*, which made a great sensation in
Europe. He became Minister of Foreign Affairs. Later he wrote
a far-sighted history *L'Ancien Régime et la Révolution* thought at
the time to be too favourable to the Revolution.

TOURIST INFORMATION 60 rue St Thomas Becket
(33.54.02.48 – in season)

HOTELS
Phare, 42 rue St-Thomas-Becket (33.54.02.07): pleasant Logis
with restaurant. ROOMS C–D. MEALS C–E. Hotel shut 10–15
March. Restaurant shut Sunday evening (low season), Monday.

BARNEVILLE CARTERET
[MANCHE]

Charming twins on the west coast of Cotentin which appeal to
three generations of holidaymakers, from small children to
grandparents. Protected by a cape and washed by the Gulf
Stream, they have a mild climate and although there is a strong
tide, bathing is good most of the time.

Carteret is delightful and very French. Local fishing boats
sell their catch on the quay and little yachts sail into the harbour
from Britain and especially from the Channel Isles. In May to
September ferry boats run from Jersey.

Barneville across the estuary from Carteret is more formal
and peaceful. There are three routes between them – a road, a

coastguard path round the headland and, at low tide, a walk across the sands. Both have beaches, with Barneville's bigger, long, clean and white. On the rocky headland, Cap Carteret, is a lighthouse open to visitors in summer.

Barneville has an 11th-century church with a 15th-century fortified tower and beautifully decorated Romanesque arches inside. On Saturdays Barneville streets are crammed with stalls selling beautiful butter and cheeses from local farms, local fish and meat and strong cider from Calvados, matured for a year.

On the way out of town is a memorial marking the cutting of the Cotentin Peninsula by American forces on 18 June 1944, when they captured Barneville, then turned north to take the vital port of Cherbourg on 26 June.

TOURIST INFORMATION 1 place Dr-Auvret, Barneville
(33.04.90.58)
ave de la République, Carteret (33.53.84.80 – high season)
MARKET Saturdays (Barneville)
FESTIVAL mid-August–Fêtes de la Mer, Carteret

HOTELS

Marine, Carteret (33.53.83.31): charming waterside inn extended, bedrooms beautifully modernised. Run by same family for four generations. Superb fresh fish, mostly landed locally. Lower-price menus outstanding value. ROOMS E–F. MEALS B (weekdays), D–G. Shut 14 November–16 December, 2 January–3 February, 23 February–2 March; restaurant shut Sunday evening, Monday October–March.
Les Isles, Barneville (33.04.90.76): comfortable, pleasant Logis above beach. Good holiday hotel. Fish direct from boats. ROOMS B–E. MEALS B–F. Shut 25 November–end January.
Hermitage-Maison-Duhamel, on port, Carteret (33.04.96.29): restaurant with studios, simple, good value; good shellfish. STUDIOS with kitchenette E–F. MEALS A–E. Shut 15 November–15 December, 4–25 January, 16 February–10 March. Restaurant shut Sunday evening, Wednesday evening.

BAYEUX
[*See Major Towns*, page 46]

BEAUMESNIL
[EURE – 13km SE of Bernay on D140]

A truly impressive Louis XIII château, its dignified 17th century façade reflected in its moat – a steep roofed ornate centre with low flanking pavilions, surrounded by formal gardens. One of the finest examples of Louis XIII style. Among rooms which can be visited are the salon with Louis XV furnishings and a museum of book-binding (open mid-April–mid-October, Friday–Monday afternoons).

BEAUMONT-EN-AUGE
[CALVADOS]

Little town with timbered houses overlooking the Touques Valley, 13km SE of Villers-sur-Mer on D118, north of the A13 motorway. 'Traditional Normandy'. Fine views from square by the church. Birthplace of the mathematician and astronomer Marquis de Laplace (1749–1827), the son of a poor tenant farmer. He became one of the world's greatest scientists and President of the French Academy, publishing many important papers on lunar and planetary science, on molecular physics, electricity and magnetism. His greatest achievements were the investigation of the tidal theory and his analytical theory of probabilities.

RESTAURANT
Abbaye (31.64.82.31): very good typically Norman auberge with Norman traditional cooking (duck or chicken in cider; Norman apple tart). MEALS D–F. Shut January; Tuesday, Wednesday.

BEAUMONT-LE-ROGER
[EURE]

In a very pretty position on the right bank of the Risle, 8km SW
of Le Neubourg in one of the richest agricultural areas of upper
Normandy. St Nicolas's church, built between the 14th and 16th
centuries, has been restored after war damage with modern
windows replacing old stained glass. There was a German airfield here. The wooden soldier Regulus still strikes the hour
from the square tower.

BEAUVOIR-EN-LYONS
[SEINE-MARITIME]

17km S Forges-les-Eaux. A pleasant little town in the Bray
region with a fine view from the church of the Bray Valley, to
Beauvais cathedral in clear weather.

LE BEC HELLOUIN
[EURE]

In 1034, the knight Herluin, tiring of battle, changed his
charger for a donkey, his armour for a monk's habit and vowed
to devote himself to God. Others joined him and eight years
later there were thirty-two monks in the Bec. In 1042 Herluin
was mending his bread oven when an Italian clerk named Lanfranc who had been teaching successfully in Avranches walked
up and asked to join. He stayed three years, then Herluin sent
him out to teach again. At the siege of nearby Brionne from
1047 to 1050, Lanfranc met young Duke William, and became
his adviser and emissary. He went to Rome to persuade the Pope
to forgive William for having married his cousin Matilda – not
too difficult, as the Pope had been Lanfranc's pupil in Italy.
Lanfranc became prior of the abbey of St Etienne at Caen. After

the Conquest of England, William made Lanfranc Archbishop of Canterbury and virtual ruler of England while the king was away warring.

Bec became the most famous school of the 11th century and its abbot Anselm, another Italian and a philosopher, succeeded Lanfranc as Archbishop of Canterbury. He was banished first by William Rufus, William the Conqueror's second son, then by King Henry I, his third son, but he returned and died as Archbishop in 1109. He is buried next to Lanfranc in Canterbury Cathedral. Another Bec graduate, Theobold, patron of Thomas à Becket, became Archbishop in 1139.

In the 17th century Bec accepted the Maurist reform (named after St Maurus), started by zealous Benedictines who believed that their order had become wayward. They repaired the abbey which became important again in Christian learning. The monks were driven out in the Revolution, the buildings became stables, then were pillaged over years and virtually destroyed. In 1809 the abbey church was pulled down and sold as scrap! The monks returned in 1948.

Le Bec Hellouin

The abbey is set in woodlands and the beautiful, elegant silvery-grey tower of St Nicolas peers at you over the trees as you approach. Built originally in 1467, it has been excellently restored, though the spire is missing. A monumental 17th-century staircase to the cloister survives. The new abbey is in the old Maurist refectory, a superbly vaulted hall. At the entrance is a 14th-century statue of the Virgin and the 11th-century Sarcophagus of Herluin himself lies before the altar, which is in Italian Aosta marble (1959). White-robed monks wander among the green lawns, well-groomed gardens and ancient fishpond (closed Tuesdays). At the entrance to the abbey in the Abbatiale is a collection of fifty cars from 1920 onwards, all in running order.

RESTAURANT WITH ROOMS
Auberge de l'Abbaye (32.44.86.02): old black-and-white Norman inn with modest bedrooms, excellent mostly Norman cooking, highish prices. Famous apple tart. ROOMS E. MEALS D–G. Shut early January–late February; Monday evening, Tuesday out of season.

BELLÊME
[ORNE]

A fine old Norman town at the top of a spur 225 metres high, overlooking the beautiful oak forest of Bellême and lovely Perche countryside.

The 15th-century ramparts have gone, apart from the city gate, Le Porche, flanked by two reconstructed towers and some other towers which are now part of houses. But Bellême keeps some of its mediaeval character, with narrow alleys and old houses with coloured shutters reflected in the old castle moat. Rue Ville-Close, built on the site of the old castle, is lined with attractive 17th and 18th-century houses. No. 26, the elegant Bansard des Bois Mansion, is outstanding. St Sauveur church is late 17th-century, pure classical, and is ornately decorated inside.

Beautiful Bellême forest, owned by the French nation, has 2400 hectares, almost all of fine oaks. Tracks and unsurfaced forestry roads make it delightful for walking, and there is a signposted route for motorists leaving Bellême by D938 and performing some contortions on its way to La Perrière and back. Part of the route is unsurfaced. It passes Étang de la Herse, a pleasant pool which you can walk round. At La Perrière, an old hilltop village, you have a magnificent panoramic view from the churchyard over the Perche.

TOURIST INFORMATION
Bellême Hôtel-de-Ville (33.73.02.21)
MARKET Thursday

HOTEL

Boule d'Or, place Gén Leclerc (33.73.10.32): very simple, useful, cheap. ROOMS A. MEALS A–B. Shut Monday.

RESTAURANT

Auberge du Tournebroche, 15 rue du Mans (33.73.11.42): is building quite a reputation for good Norman cooking (salmon; duck in cider). MEALS B–D. Shut Monday evening, Tuesday.

BÉNERVILLE-SUR-MER
and
BLONVILLE-SUR-MER
[CALVADOS]

Twin resorts, virtually joined, only 4km SW of Deauville, at foot of Mount Canisty. Gently sloping, long sandy beach lures families. A cheaper place to stay when visiting Deauville.

HOTEL

De la Mer, 93 ave République (31.87.93.23): nice little holiday hotel. No restaurant. ROOMS B–E. Shut 1 November–31 March.

RESTAURANTS
Éscale, place Hôtel-de-Ville (31.87.93.56): large restaurant renowned for good straightforward Norman cooking of fine fresh fish. Excellent shellfish platter. MEALS B–F. Shut 23 November–28 December; Monday evening, Tuesday, Wednesday.
Ferme du Bois Lauret, 2.5km S by D118, right turn after the station (31.87.42.62): in countryside on large farm with horse-stud. 'Elaborate classical' cooking. MEALS C–F. Shut 6 January–15 February; Wednesday; Thursday (October–May).

BÉNOUVILLE
[CALVADOS – *see* D-Day, page 57 and Caen, page 40]

BERNAY
[EURE]

A handsome and historic town where the river Charentonne meets the Cosnier. Here in the 12th century the troubadour Alexandre de Bernay developed the twelve-syllable iambic line in poetry, called the Alexandrine. The 11th-century abbey, mostly rebuilt by the Maurists in the 17th century, is now the town hall. The old abbey church was begun in 1013 by da Volpiano from Fécamp abbey. It has been restored after being shamefully abandoned. (Shut Tuesday; mornings in winter except Wednesday.)

Many of Bernay's roads contain old half-timbered houses, including a former 16th-century logis of the abbey, now the municipal museum. A good collection of French and Dutch paintings, pottery of Rouen, Delft and Nevers, and old Norman furniture. Worth seeing. (Opening times as abbey church.) Ste Croix (Church of the Holy Cross) is 14th century, heavily restored. It contains some 15th-century statues rescued from Bec Hellouin abbey, and tombstones, notably the remarkable stone of Guillaume d'Auvilliers, Abbot of Bec (1418).

TOURIST INFORMATION Hôtel-de-Ville (32.43.32.08)
MARKET Saturday
FESTIVALS Religious procession Monday of Pentecost
FLOWER FESTIVAL end March–early April

HOTELS

Angleterre et Cheval Blanc, rue de Gaulle (32.43.11.75): Logis long renowned for Norman cooking of local farm produce. Three dining rooms of different styles. Edward VII stayed when Prince of Wales. ROOMS B–C. MEALS C–F. Shut 15 January–1 February.

Hostellerie du Moulin Fouret, 4km S at St Aubin-le-Vertueux (32.43.19.95): in ravishing old mill by Charentonne river François Deduit, formerly with Guérard, cooks meals of outstanding value, full of ideas. Try *sole à la crème orange*. ROOMS B–C. MEALS C–F. Shut 22 December–15 January, mid-August–early September; Monday except from 1 May–mid-August.

BERNIÈRES-SUR-MER
[CALVADOS – *see also* D-Day page 57]

Little family seaside resort 19km NW of Ouistreham with a beach where low tide reveals a reef along which fishermen net shrimps and crabs. Here the French-Canadian 'Chaudière' Division landed on D-Day with press and radio correspondents. Bernières has a beautiful church with a spire 67 metres high and a Romanesque tower which, incredibly, has survived intact since the 11th century. It has four successive receding storeys with bays. A door above ground level is reached by a ladder which could be drawn up after people had sought refuge in the upper storeys from invading enemies.

MARKET Wednesday

BEUVRON-EN-AUGE
[CALVADOS]

Showpiece village and 'Sauvegarde' (protected site), with everything lovingly painted and cleaned. Old mansions, covered market and craft shops. A little like a film set but pleasant. It is on
the Route des Cidres 13km S of Dives-sur-Mer.

FESTIVAL around 20 November – Cider Festival

RESTAURANT

Le Pavé d'Auge (31.79.26.71): my favourite French gastronome
Marc de Champérard is lyrical in the praises of Odile Engel
from Alsace. Michelin gives her a star. Gault-Millau gives her
two 'toques' and a very high 16 out of 20 and they are all right! If
you want to taste dishes using brilliantly all the delights of
Normandy, here is the place – mussels, oysters and fish, lambs,
chickens, ducks, fresh vegetables, triple cream and butter,
cheeses, cider, apples and calvados. Try her *soupe de moules au
cidre* (mussels in cider), *poêlée d'huitres en cidre* (oysters in cider),
canard au pommes (duck in cider, apples and cream) or *poulet
fermier vallée d'Auge* (a superb version of the famous chicken in
Calvados and cream). Lovely apple tart. Magnificent very old
calvados – at a price. MEALS D–G. Shut Monday evening, Tuesday (check by phone, seasonal variations); mid-January–end
February.

BEUZEVILLE
[EURE]

Market town just north of A13 motorway, 15km S of Honfleur.
The 13th to 16th-century church has fine modern windows by
the Norman artist Décorchemont (1880–1971). Strategically
placed for Deauville (23km), Honfleur (15km), Pont Audemer
(14km), Le Havre (48km), Caen (51km).

MARKET Tuesday

HOTELS

Cochon d'Or et Petit Castel, place Gén. de Gaulle (32.57.70.46): old-style cooking *sole normande*, super *poulet vallée d'Auge*, duck in orange sauce, good desserts. Simple rooms in old Cochon, more modern in Petit Castel 50 metres away. ROOMS B–E. MEALS A–F. Shut 15 December–15 January. Cochon shut Mondays.

Auberge de la Hauquerie at Quetteville, 3km W of Beuzeville on N175 (31.64.14.46): Simone Lombard runs hotel-restaurant with good regional cooking and individual ideas while her husband schools horses. ROOMS D–F. MEALS B–D. Shut Christmas–30 December; 10 January–15 February; Thursday except July, August.

BIÉVILLE-SUR-ORNE
[CALVADOS]

5km NE Caen by D60. Village with unusual Italian-style church with blind arcades. Hilltop view northwards to the sea and to Ouistreham belfry. Attractive countryside.

BLAINVILLE
[SEINE-MARITIME]

Village in the Crevon valley 20km NE of Rouen which has an attractive collegiate church of 1488 faced in a chequered pattern of sandstone and silex. Inside is an interesting 15th-century wood statue of St Michael. Ruins of a mediaeval château were found in 1968, with an 11th-century staircase, a long curtain wall and two 14th to 15th-century towers.

BLANGY-SUR-BRESLE
[Seine-Maritime]

Very busy little market town rebuilt since World War Two. Not pretty, but vital. On the edge of the delightful Eu forest of groves of beeches and oaks with marked paths for walking and little roads for driving.

MARKETS Friday; 3rd Wednesday of each month

HOTEL
Auberge du Tivoli, 1 route Neufchatel (35.93.51.16): very simple; cheap good value menus. ROOMS A–C. MEALS A–C. Restaurant closed Sunday evening low season.

LA BOUILLE
[Seine-Maritime]

This little village on the Seine's rocky south bank just south of Rouen must have been absolutely delightful when Monet came here to paint. Considering the invasion of Rouen's citizens on fine weekends, it has survived remarkably well and is very pretty. A hamlet with half-timbered old houses where Seine barges still stop for their crews to leap ashore to shop, it has three hotels and very good restaurants, packed with Rouennais at Sunday lunchtime. A small car ferry (*bac*) takes you to the wooded north bank of the Seine where there is a road to Rouen.

Above the bend in the river towards the A13 motorway, are the remains of the castle of Robert le Diable (Robert the Devil), Duke of Normandy, father of William the Conqueror by a tanner's daughter, Arlette. In the Hundred Years War, the French blew it up to stop the English taking it and now its ruins are pleasure grounds for tourists.

HOTELS
Le Saint-Pierre (35.23.80.10): delightful ambience, charming wel-

come from Giselle and Bernard Huet. Seine-side terrace, superb dishes of young Patrice Kukurudz, one of the best young chefs in France. He chooses ingredients with utmost care, cooks lightly but with regional emphasis (superb duck) and avoids the bland tastelessness of modern cooking. Good wine list. ROOMS E–F. MEALS D–G. Shut Tuesday evening; Wednesday from 1 November–31 March.

RESTAURANT
Maison Blanche, 1 quai Hector Malot (35.23.80.53): big, attractive house overlooking Seine, beautifully decorated with old-style Norman furniture and cooking. Good fish. MEALS C–F. Shut mid-July–early August, 19 December–4 January; Sunday evening, Monday.

BOURG DUN
[SEINE-MARITIME]

Not many tourists go out of their way to see a village church but this one just 6km NE of the delightful little seaside resort of Veules-les-Roses is worth the trouble. Its mixture of architectural styles makes it look like a family château, mainly because of its tower built on a 13th-century base. The 17th-century roof is axe-shaped. Inside, beneath Flamboyant vaulting, is a Renaissance bay, three wide bays of the chancel from the 14th century and lovely 16th-century font. The village inn is simple and charming.

RESTAURANT
Auberge du Dun (35.83.05.84): excellent food cooked by a very good chef at reasonable prices. MEALS B–F. Shut mid-October–early November, Christmas, 15 February–5 March; Sunday evening, Monday.

BOURG-ST-LEONARD
[ORNE]

Hamlet near Haras du Pin (Le Pin stud), east of Argentan. A beautifully elegant and harmonious Louis XV château well worth visiting when seeing Château d'O and the Haras. Like so many fine houses in France, it was built by a Royal financial official – Jules Gromot, Commissioner to the Controller General of Finance. The interior woodwork, furniture and tapestries are of rare quality, much unchanged from the original. It was the scene of great 'fêtes galantes', theatrical performances and balls. (Open beginning of May–mid-September except Tuesday.)

BRACQUEMENT
[SEINE-MARITIME]

On D113 just NE of Dieppe. Church with unusually brilliant stained glass windows by Henderycksen.

BRETEUIL-SUR-ITON
[EURE]

Nice market town almost surrounded by an arm of the river Iton in lovely area between Risle valley and Ouche country. It backs onto the Breteuil forest and close by forest of Conches. The river forms a pool bordered by very pleasant public gardens on the site of an ancient fort. Oldest part of the Romanesque church dates from William the Conqueror. Here William's daughter Adèle married Étienne, Count of Blois. Their son Stephen became King of England.

HOTEL
Mail, rue Neuve-de-Bémécourt (32.29.81.54): charming 18th-

century Norman house, old beamed rooms, pleasant garden. Calm and tranquil. Good reputation for cuisine. ROOMS D–F. MEALS C–E. Shut mid-November–1 December; Monday from November–February.

RESTAURANT

Le Biniou, 76 place Lafitte (32.29.70.61): grill; good value; very good fish; charcoal. Town centre. MEALS A–E. Shut part January; Tuesday evening, Wednesday.

BRICQUEBEC
[MANCHE]

Interesting little town of character built around the remains of a 14th-century castle, it is an excellent stopping place in preference to Cherbourg. The castle's surviving inner courtyard has

Bricquebec Castle

the Vieux Château Hotel built into it. Climb the 160 steps to the upper platform of the 14th-century keep (23 metres) for fine views of the town, countryside and the monastery (open July–August; other times apply at Hôtel de Ville). Henry V gave the castle to the Duke of Suffolk after Agincourt, but he gave it back to the French later as part of his ransom after capture by Joan of Arc in 1429. Queen Victoria stayed in the hotel in 1857 after visiting Cherbourg for the opening of the railway to Caen. A good market is held before the castle gates on Mondays. The Trappist monastery (Abbaye Notre-Dame-de-Grâce), 3km along D121, was founded in 1824. Men and women may enter the monastery and the church at 3.30 p.m. except Sundays and holidays.

MARKET Monday

HOTEL

Vieux Château (33.52.24.49): Hubert Hardy's little hotel has unusual and delightful atmosphere. Good value; good regional cooking. Bedrooms improved but vary in size and comfort. ROOMS B–E. MEALS A–E. Shut 20 December–25 February.

BRIONNE
[EURE]

A pleasant market town on islands where the Risle divides into channels, it is a good place for an overnight stay or as a touring centre. Only 6km from the once powerful Bec-Hellouin monastery (page 84), it was in mediaeval times a stronghold commanding the Risle valley. While besieging it, William the Conqueror met the monk Lanfranc, who had such an influence on his life and on England's history. You can see the ruins of the 11th-century donjon, with views from an orientation table. Maison de Normandie, a typical old Norman house, contains an exhibition and shop of Norman crafts and agricultural products. (Shut Wednesday except in summer.) The church of St Martin has a 17th-century marble altar from Bec-Hellouin, 14th-century

Gothic wood vaulting, and modern stained glass by Gabriel Loire of Chartres.

MARKET Thursday

HOTEL

Logis de Brionne, place St Denis (32.44.81.73). Regional dishes following markets and season. Very good fish. Most rooms improved recently. ROOMS A–C. MEALS B–F. Shut 24 December–23 January; Sunday evening; Monday (except evening in high season).

BROGLIE
[EURE]

Little town 11km S Bernay on N138 is beside the Charentonne river. Once called Chambrais but its name was changed to Broglie (pronounced Bro'-y) when a princely family from Piedmont took over in 1716 and altered the mediaeval château. It still dominates the town and still belongs to the Broglie family, who have distinguished themselves in many spheres. Victor François (1718–1804) was the most capable French general in the Seven Years War against Marlborough. Achille was a Liberal politician who led a fight in France for the abolition of slavery and was Prime Minister of France under King Louis-Philippe (1835–6). Jacques-Victor (1821–1901) was an accomplished writer, ambassador to London and twice Prime Minister (1873, 1877). Maurice (1875–1960) was a physician famed for his research into X-ray and his younger brother Louis, a physicist, won a Nobel prize in 1929 for pioneer work on the undulatory theory of matter.

RESTAURANT

Poste (32.44.60.18): MEALS C–F. Shut 1–12 October, 14–28 December; Monday evening, Tuesday.

BROTONNE FOREST
[Seine-Maritime]

The massive and handsome toll bridge which crosses the Seine
from Caudebec on the north bank is fifty metres above the water
and 1280 metres long. It takes you to the village of St Nicolas de
Bliquetuit then into the Brotonne forest, a delightful retreat of
beeches, oaks and pines with pleasant views along forest roads
and tracks.

At Vatteville on D65, a pretty road by the river W of the
forest, is a 17th-century mill and a church with beautiful 15th to
16th-century windows. At La Haye-du-Routot are two massive
yew trees 16 and 14 metres round. One contains a chapel, the
other an oratory. They are hundreds of years old. The forest of
7400 hectares was once a royal hunting ground and a huge old
house near Vatteville was used by François I. In the 16th century, Vatteville was a port with two hundred boats going to the
Newfoundland banks. They cut down great oaks for the ships
and the forest was not replanted until last century. Since 1974
the forest has been part of the Parc Naturel Régional de Brotonne, on both banks of the Seine, covering 42,000 hectares.

FESTIVAL at La Haye-du-Routot on the night of 16–17
July a huge fire is lit. People pull huge brands from it as
a symbol of defence against fire (*Le Feu de St Clair*)

BRUNEVAL
[Seine-Maritime]

Not even marked on most maps any more. Bureaucrats have
joined this hamlet with its traditional rival Saint Jouin. Drive
4½km on D940 S of Étretat, turn right 3km to a beach and you
see a memorial. It commemorates an incredibly successful raid
by British parachutists on the night of 27–28 February 1942.
With the help of French Resistance fighters they landed, and
within ten minutes destroyed the German positions, and stole
new secret radar equipment. Then they got away safely in Royal

Navy boats under the command of Lord Mountbatten. Two Britons were killed, three taken prisoner. It was such an important operation that Churchill gave it half a page in his war history. Now you can see a huge breakwater which protects an oil-tanker port called Havre-Antifer built in 1976. Not so ugly as it sounds, for the oil storage tanks hide under a cliff. It was built to take supertankers of 500,000 tonnes. Le Havre could take tankers up to 250,000 tonnes. The changing world of oil has already cut its trade to about three dozen ships a year.

CABOURG and DIVES-SUR-MER
[CALVADOS]

Cabourg was built up as a fashionable seaside resort at the time of the Second Empire and is a delightful vignette of those starry-eyed days. Despite new, low blocks of efficient, square holiday apartments, the break-up of big, old houses into holiday flats, and barely tolerable crowds of cars in its shopping centre in mid-summer, it keeps some of its atmosphere and much of its elegance. It is still '*très gentil*', like a genteel old lady, still active and pleasant.

Cabourg was planned with geometric symmetry. Its main avenues radiate in half circles from Boulevard des Anglais, a terrace running above enormous fine sands. In the very centre of the central promenade are the Casino and the truly grand and very white Grand Hotel, with its ornate entrance in the Jardin du Casino square, its beach and restaurant entrance on the promenade. The promenade itself is now called after Marcel Proust and indeed the writer stayed often in the Grand Hotel. He used the scenes on the sands and promenade in his book *A l'Ombre des Jeunes Filles en Fleur* (*Within a Budding Grove*) calling Cabourg 'Balbeck'. His descriptions of beach scenes make it difficult to believe the story that he virtually hid away until after dark and dined alone after other diners had finished. Perhaps he spied on Albertine playing with her diabolo on the breakwater from his bedroom window.

Cabourg was not damaged in World War Two and its

avenues are still lined with the original ornate little Norman houses, many hiding primly behind lime trees. It is a pity that the centre around Jardin du Casino is not kept as a pedestrian area – or for the horse-drawn carriages you can still hire to add atmosphere to your visit. It is very appropriate that Proust should have written here *A la Recherche du Temps Perdu* (*Remembrance of Things Past*).

Dives-sur-Mer, twice the size of Cabourg, faces it across the Dives river. Its historic great port has long since silted up and the main town is 2km inland. It is semi-industrial, with a copper-alloy works. But it still has a fishing port and now a marina used by yachtsmen. But, once ashore, they make for Cabourg. Dives was the first scene in an act which changed the history of the world.

On 12 September 1066, under the standard not of William the Bastard, Duke of Normandy, but of the Pope, 695 ships took aboard 12,000 knights and footsoldiers and, followed by another fleet of boats and skiffs – 3000 vessels in all, sailed to St Valery-sur-Somme to pick up reinforcements, then on to England. They landed at Pevensey in Sussex.

In Dives today there still exists the 11th-century transept crossing in the 14th to 15th-century church of Notre Dame de Dives. On a list carved in 1862 of the names of the lords who crossed with William, many names may seem familiar.

The superb timber roof of Dives' 15th to 16th-century market is still intact. Alas, the lovely 16th-century Hostellerie de Guillaume le Conquérant, an alluring inn where such celebrities as Alexandre Dumas, Mme de Sévigné and the statesman and writer Thiers stayed, has been rebuilt and turned into a craft centre and flats. A restaurant survives.

TOURIST INFORMATION Tourist Office, Jardin du Casino, Cabourg (31.91.01.09)

MARKET Cabourg – daily in summer; Wednesday, Friday in winter

FESTIVALS July – 1000 Sails Regatta. Late August – William the Conqueror Festival with parade and floats

HOTELS

Pullman Grand Hotel, Cabourg (31.91.01.79): *see above*; still very grand with marble halls. Restaurant called Le Balbec. Even a *Thé Dansant*. Imaginative dishes, some classic, but I should have preferred *Grande Cuisine* in such a grand setting. Rooms luxurious and expensive. MEALS E–F. Open all year.

Le Cottage, 24 ave Gén. Leclerc (31.91.65.61): charming Norman-style house-hotel. No restaurant. ROOMS C–D. Open all year.

L'Oie qui Fume, 18 ave la Brèche Buhot (31.91.27.79): This smoking goose lives in a Logis de France. ROOMS B–D. MEALS A–D. Shut 4 January–4 February; Sunday evening, Monday, Tuesday in winter.

Moulin du Pré, at Bavent, 7km SW, route Gonneville-en-Auge (31.78.83.68): becoming popular with gastronomes. Good shellfish and duck dishes. Restored mill with charming little rooms. Garden with lake and stream. ROOMS B–D. MEALS F–G. Shut first fortnight March, October; Sunday night, Monday except July, August.

RESTAURANT

Guillaume-le-Conquérant, at Dives, 2 rue Hastings (31.91.07.26): in stables of 16th-century, former coaching inn. Fish landed locally. MEALS D–G. Shut December; Tuesday evening, Wednesday except July–August.

CAEN
[*see Major Towns*, page 40]

CAMEMBERT
[CALVADOS]

Village 5km SW of Vimoutiers where the farmer's wife, Marie Harel improved the Auge soft cheese now named after the village and sent it to market in Vimoutiers. She was helped by a priest she was hiding from the Revolution (*see* Cheeses, page 11). She deserves the statue in her village in honour of what she has done for France. Ninety per cent of cheese made in Calvados is now camembert, but not all cheese called camembert comes from Calvados.

CANAPVILLE
[CALVADOS]

Alas, you must apply in writing to see one of the most beautiful manor houses in Normandy – the 13th to 15th-century manor of the Bishops of Lisieux (Manoir des Évêques de Lisieux, Canapville, 14800 Deauville). In the attractive valley of the river Touques, with orchards and pastures along its east bank, the manor is 5km S of Deauville. It is built of wood, with three beautiful stone chimneys around a staircase tower. Well worth seeing from outside. This is a good place to stay for visiting Deauville.

HOTELS

Hostellerie de l'Aubergade, route de Paris (31.65.22.59): most attractive old farm lying back from the road in its own little park. Comfortable with lots of atmosphere. Old-style regional cooking, with very good gastronomic menu. ROOMS B–E. MEALS B–G. Shut January–end of March; Wednesday.

Auberge de la Truite at St-Martin-aux-Chartrains, 3km S Canapville on N177, 2½km from Pont l'Évêque (31.65.21.64): old Norman house became a village inn in 1900. The little Douet river in its garden is polluted – the trout have gone. Young Jean-Michel Lebon and wife Françoise serve modern regional dishes such as *lotte* (monkfish) in cider, beautifully presented. Some of *Les Planches* brigade (the fashionable visitors) from Deauville come here for a touch of rusticity. Menu prices are reasonable, carte prices are 'Deauvillais'. Rooms are rustic. ROOMS B–D. MEALS C–G. Shut February; Wednesday evening, Thursday except in August.

CARENTAN
[MANCHE]

A Roman town at the meeting of the Taute and Douve rivers and gateway to the Cotentin, it is now an important cattle market town and a dairy centre. Its small harbour at the end of the deep inlet of the Taute river has become a pleasure boat centre, and further along the inlet Douves river reaches the sea. The town is dominated by the huge 12th to 15th-century Notre Dame church, whose octagonal spire can be seen sometimes for great distances. The covered market with attractive arcades in place de la République is 14th century. The elegant town hall (17th to 19th centuries) was once a convent.

TOURIST INFORMATION Syndicat d'Initiative, Hôtel-de-Ville (33.42.33.54)

HOTEL
Commerce et de la Gare, facing railway station, place Valnoble (33.42.02.00): old-style auberge offering traditional meals, well cooked, at low prices. ROOMS (simple) C–D. MEALS A–C. Shut 22 December–22 January, 1–10 October; Friday; Sunday evening.

RESTAURANT
Auberge Normande, 17 boul. Verdun (33.42.02.99): Gérard Bonnefoy is a great chef who lightens regional dishes and invents his own. MEALS C(weekdays)–G. Shut Sunday evening, Monday.

CAROLLES
[MANCHE]

Village perched on a headland on Cotentin coast. Just N of Mont-St-Michel bay, with sandy beach at the bottom of a cliff. Round the headland are huge stretches of sand at low tide. Carolles still has a 19th-century ambience – a promenade with villas and gardens, backed by woodland walks. But relics of

German defences do mix incongruously with the 12th-century village church inland.

HOTEL

Relais de la Diligence (33.61.86.42): unbelievable! Alain Duval's two cheaper menus must be the best bargains in Normandy. His expensive menu would not disgrace a smart restaurant. Real cheap French holiday hotel. ROOMS (simple) A–B. MEALS A, C, G. Shut January, February; Sunday evening, Monday low season.

CARROUGES
[ORNE]

This hamlet on the D908 between the Écouves and Andaine forests, east of La Ferté-Macé, belongs to the Normandy Maine Regional Nature Park. It is the park's headquarters. Maison du Parc is in the outbuildings of the castle. Here you can get information about outdoor activities in the park's 233,908 hectares. The village was fortified by the Counts of Carrouges in the 12th century but passed to the powerful Veneur family, Counts of Tillières, in 1450 and they held it until 1936.

The castle is one of the finest in France and would be much better known if it were in the Loire or Dordogne. It is vast, built in rose-red brick and grey granite with a surrounding moat and looks superb in its setting beside the river Udon.

Most of the present castle was built in the 16th century under Henri IV. Even the entrance gateway is a beautifully proportioned miniature château, and the stone balustrade round the moat is beautiful. The castle is elegant but strong, and superbly proportioned with definite lines, but not dull, for the corner towers are square and octagonal, its steep Norman roof broken by dormer windows. But it is the clever use of colouring in the materials which is so striking. From the blue-grey roof, the towers are in deep rose-red, shading subtly down to the grey-granite of the stone dipping into the moat.

Fine ornate iron gates with floral designs lead to a formal

Gatehouse, Château Carrouges

terrace-garden high above the fields and woods, and avenues of chestnuts lead through Renaissance gateways to the tranquil woods and fields. Inside is a very fine stairway, state rooms decorated in a mixture of classical and Renaissance styles, rare furniture and a renowned portrait gallery. (Castle shut Tuesdays except mid-June to end August.)

HOTEL

St Pierre, place Mairie (33.27.20.02): Logis – village inn; tea room, too. ROOMS B–C. MEALS A–E. Shut February; Wednesday.

CARTERET
[*see* Barneville, page 81]

CAUDEBEC-EN-CAUX
[SEINE-MARITIME]

Once an important little port on the Seine, with a much-used ferry, and gems of mediaeval houses, Caudebec was terribly damaged in 1940 when the Germans deliberately set fire to it. Then the huge graceful Brotonne bridge was built just upstream in 1977 and Caudebec has settled down to its new role of market town and small tourist centre. Undamaged was the superb Flamboyant church of Notre Dame, built between 1425 and 1539 when the English ruled here and described later by Henri IV as 'the most beautiful chapel in the kingdom'. Certainly the rich delicacy of its carvings, the beauty of its belfry tower and octagonal spire, its magnificent Flamboyant doorways and rose window surrounded by small statues are quite breathtaking in such an unassuming little town.

The stained glass is a joy, too, though not all 15th century, for some had to be replaced last century. Some of the windows are Flemish, some made locally and those above the north door came from England, a gift of Captain Eyton, last English commander here in the Hundred Years War (1435–47). These show St George, St Catherine, St Michael and the Virgin. The choir stalls and Louis XIII woodwork came from the old abbey of St Wandrille (*see below*). Large stone statues in the Chapel of the Holy Sepulchre are from Jumièges abbey. This chapel, which contains a 15th-century *Pietà*, so impressed the 18th-century artist Fragonard that he painted it. The great organ with 2,300 pipes is world famous.

Two mediaeval houses survived the fire, with Maison des Templiers, of which two 13th-century gable walls still stand. The interior, much altered, has a small local history museum. The Saturday market in place du Marché dates from 1390.

At the west end of the promenade opposite the town hall terrace (good river view) is a new museum of Seine navigation, with some interesting wooden boats.

St Wandrille's abbey, 4km east, was founded in AD 649 under the name of Fontenelle, a little river which ran through its grounds. It was ruined in the Revolution but the monks returned in 1931 and built anew. All that remains of the old abbey are some tall columns, and bases of the church and all four galleries of the cloister. The new church is in a 15th-century tithe barn (Canteloup Barn) brought here in pieces from the Eure in 1969 and re-erected. In it you can hear the Gregorian Chant (9.25 a.m. on weekdays, 10 a.m. on Sunday). The Abbey cloisters open afternoons; also Sunday morning. Count Wandrille founded the abbey. He was so physically splendid that he was called 'God's True Athlete'. A count at the court of King Dagobert in the 7th century, he was celebrating his wedding when he and his bride vowed to stick to pure love and parted to become a monk and a nun. His abbey grew over two centuries into one of the great abbey schools and libraries, with learned abbots, and produced so many saints that this became known as the Valley of the Saints.

In the 19th century the abbey became a textile mill, then was bought by an English peer, the Marquess of Stacpole, who did much to renovate it, using it as a home. Then it became the home of Maurice Maeterlinck, Belgian dramatist, author of *Life of a Bee*, one of the first popular dramatisations of a scientific subject.

A short distance from the abbey, at the edge of the abbey porch, is St Saturnin Chapel, built in the 10th century. It was given a new facade in the 16th century but still has a heavy square tower, with three side chapels. The inside is restored, with interesting pillars decorated with roses, palms and strange animals at the top.

TOURIST INFORMATION Caudebec Syndicat d'Initiative, pl. Charles de Gaulle (1 April–1 November – 35.96.20.65); La Mairie (2 November–March – 35.96.11.12)

MARKET Saturday morning

FESTIVALS Cider Festival – last Sunday in September, every two years.

Boat trips on Seine in summer

Manoir de Retival

HOTELS

Manoir de Rétival, rue St Clair (35.96.11.22): creeper-clad 19th-century manor in lovely garden with views; tastefully furnished with antiques; peaceful. No restaurant. ROOMS G. Shut 2 November–15 March.

Normandie, 19 quai Guilbaud (35.96.25.11): opposite river; good value; old-style regional cooking; good choice; very popular. ROOMS C–E. MEALS A (weekdays), C–E. Shut February; restaurant shut Sunday evening.

Marine, 18 quai Guilbaud (35.96.20.11): more formal than Normandie. Soundproofed from quayside traffic. Comfortable. ROOMS C–E. MEALS B(weekdays)–F. Shut mid-December–mid-January; Sunday evening in winter.

RESTAURANT

Auberge Deux Couronnes, at St Wandrille (35.96.11.44): restaurant in old Norman house opposite abbey. Good value. MEALS C–D. Shut 5–23 September; end January–9 February; Sunday evening, Monday.

CÉRISY-LA-FORÊT
[MANCHE]

A narrow road through a thick beech forest where deer roam, leads from Balleroy (*see* page 79) to this hamlet with an impressive 11th-century abbey. Though the nave is reduced to three of its original eight bays, its height and lofty pillars have an immediate and surprising impact. Great arcades are topped by a gallery, but it is simplicity which produces its effect.

There are restored 13th-century buildings, a Gothic Abbot's chapel, remains of a dungeon with prisoners' graffiti from the 15th to 16th centuries, a Judgement Room (Presidial) with a small museum of furniture and documents, and a disappointing Lapidary Museum with pieces of statues (open daily in summer, Sunday rest of year).

CHAMP DE BATAILLE CHÂTEAU
[EURE]

Massive but harmonious and lovely 17th-century manor house of pink brick and stone, 10km SE of Brionne, set in a deer park and built around a huge courtyard garden. It was pillaged in the Revolution. The Harcourt family now own it again and have refurnished it tastefully, with many *objets d'art*. Fine panelling and period chimney-pieces, Gobelin tapestries, paintings by Drouais, Van Loo and Fragonard and many good sculptures, including works by Pigalle and Canova. Pleasant park with wild rhododendrons and old trees. Open mid-March–mid-November, except Tuesday.

LA CHAPELLE-MONTLIGEON
[Orne]

Hamlet SW of Mortagne-au-Perche built originally around a Renaissance church but early this century a huge Neo-Gothic pilgrimage basilica was built with modern stained glass windows.

CHAUSEY ISLANDS
[Manche]

All but one of these isles, islets and reefs off the Cotentin coast are uninhabited. Boats take visitors from Granville in summer. According to tradition, they were once part of the Seissy forest, submerged by the sea in 709. Brown granite quarried here was used to build Mont-St-Michel Abbey. The quarries are no longer worked, but about a hundred people live on Grande Île in summer. It is only 2km long and 700 metres across at its widest. most of the people are fishermen and their families, and they return to the mainland in winter, leaving about six people behind. There is a fort built between 1860 and 1866 in case the British attacked the coast, a lighthouse 37 metres high which is not open to the public and an old fort from 1558, also not open, which was reconstructed in 1923 as a fortress-home of Louis Renault, the car manufacturer, when kidnapping of members of millionaires' families for ransom was fashionable. A small fishermen's chapel has six modern stained glass windows depicting fishing life. An aileron from a US plane shot down on 8 June 1944 stands as a memorial to the liberation of Normandy.

CHERBOURG
[*see Major Towns*, page 50]

CLÉCY
[Calvados]

A delightful little town above a great curve in the river Orne at the foot of wooded slopes, it is an excellent centre for exploring the beauty spots of the Suisse-Normande, for cycling and walking through peaceful woodlands, for canoeing, boating or fishing. Along the river bank beside Pont de Vey has grown up a line of summer cafés and restaurants where you can eat in the open or under roof-shelters, and there are a few touristy shops selling craft souvenirs (pottery, engravings on wood, etc.). There is a canoeing club and school, with shallow rapids and a little river island. Over the bridge, with lawns down to the balustrade above the river, is an old water-mill, almost hidden in creeper and roses. Denise Leduc has turned Moulin du Vey into one of the most seductive country hotels in France (*see* hotels).

A half-kilometre walk from the bridge brings you to Manoir de Placy, a 16th-century manor house made into a museum of old farming machinery and implements, antique furniture and 19th-century Bayeux porcelain. In Clécy is a superb model-railway museum, with tracks and scenery, stations, houses, replica of a route from here to Flanders. Good local walks include one signposted to Croix de la Faverie, from between the church and post office (lovely view over river and railway viaduct to Rochers des Parcs). Another walk follows footpath GR36 from the little church at Le Vey to Le Pain du Sucre, from where you have a superb panorama over the river Orne.

TOURIST INFORMATION Mairie (31.69.71.47)

HOTELS
Moulin du Vey, Le Vey (31.69.71.08): *see* above. One of our favourite country hideouts. Fine furnishings, superb position by

river Orne. Imaginative cooking by *la patronne*'s son-in-law, Michel Choplin. ROOMS E–F. MEALS C–G. Shut end November–27 December; 4–31 January. Restaurant shut Friday lunchtime in winter. *Annexe* (bed and breakfast) 3km – Relais de Surosne.

Site Normand, place l'Église (31.69.71.05): after forty years Mme Foucher still provides very good regional cooking; outstanding value. ROOMS B–D. MEALS B–E. Shut January, February; Monday in winter.

RESTAURANT

Auberge du Chalet, at Cantepie, on edge of Clécy (31.69.71.10): Patrick Charpentier's attractive auberge is renowned for classical and regional dishes. Cheap menus are excellent value. MEALS B–E. Shut 15 January–15 February.

CLÈRES
[SEINE-MARITIME]

In the grounds of a 14th-century château, largely reconstructed in the 19th century, is a famous zoo founded in 1920 by naturalist Jean Delacour, technical director of New York Zoo. He opened it to the public in 1947. It specialises in birds, including 450 species of water fowl on its lake, pink flamingoes, Oriental geese, storks, peacocks. In one area deer, wallabies, antelope and kangaroos peer at you through the trees, and Indo-Chinese gibbons from an islet in the lake. (Shut early December–early March.) A pleasant village, with a stream running through, village inns and 15th to 16th-century half-timbered houses. Rather crowded in summer.

Opposite the old timber-covered market is a most interesting automobile museum, with vehicles from a steam fire engine of 1876 to the present, including a Panhard-Levassor of 1894 and old motorcycles, pre-1900 bicycles, and *voiturettes*; also tanks, armoured cars and aircraft from Two World Wars. (Open daily except from 15 November–1 March, when it closes on Sunday.) At Bocasse, 2km W on D6, is a children's amusement park with picnic areas (open mid-May–early September, and school holidays in spring and autumn).

COLLEVILLE-MONTGOMERY PLAGE
[Calvados]

Beach just west of Ouistreham where the 4th Anglo-French Commando landed at dawn on D-Day. The town added the name of General Montgomery, British Commander-in-Chief of Ground Forces on D-Day, to its name and put up a statue to him. His family originated in Normandy. Good bathing beach.

RESTAURANT
La Ferme Saint-Hubert, 3 rue de la Mer (31.96.35.41): huge choice including five menus. Classical cooking, slightly modernised. MEALS A–G. Shut 24 December–5 January; Sunday evening, Monday.

COLLEVILLE-SUR-MER
[Calvados]

Just inland from Omaha Beach (*see* page 61). Last Germans were not driven from the village church until 10 a.m. 7 June 1944. Church is now completely rebuilt. Nearest village to the huge American Military Cemetery where 9385 crosses in Carrara marble mark the graves.

CONCHES-EN-OUCHE
[Eure]

Perched attractively on a spur almost encircled by the river Rouloir among woodlands, the town is known for the superb Renaissance windows of Ste Foy church, dating from early 16th century. Those in the north aisle show the life of the Virgin. Seven windows in the chancel are 10.5 metres high and show the life of Christ and of Ste Foy. They are believed to have been inspired by the great German engraver Dürer, and made by Romain Buron of Beauvais. Among the south aisle windows is the splendid Mystical Wine Press. Alabaster triptyches showing the Passion and the Holy Trinity were by 15th-century English craftsmen.

Conches was called Douville. Then Roger I, Lord of Conches, joined a Christian Crusade in the 11th century to fight the Moors in Spain, made a pilgrimage to Conques-en-Rouergues to the relics of the child Ste Foy, stole them, took them home to Douville, built a church to the saint and renamed the town. His church was replaced by the present Gothic building in the 15th century.

A little garden behind the town hall contains ruins of a 12th-century castle which was abandoned after the Protestants of Evreux took it in the 15th century. Pleasant main street.

TOURIST INFORMATION Hôtel de Ville (32.30.23.15)
MARKET Thursday

HOTEL

La Grand'Mare, 13 ave Croix-de-Fer (32.30.23.30): old black-and-white *Logis* overlooking lake went through a bad patch. Now run by two young professionals. Simple, cheap rooms. Classic cooking of seasonal fresh food. Good value. ROOMS A–D. MEALS C–G. Shut February; Sunday evening, Monday October–March.

RESTAURANT

La Toque Blanche, 18 place Carnot (32.30.01.54): very Norman; old Norman building, great old Norman dishes, including fish; farm cheeses. Calvados selection 10 to 100 years old. Auge cider, perry from Domfront. Staff dressed in Norman costume. MEALS C–F. Shut Monday, Tuesday evening.

CONDÉ-SUR-NOIREAU
[CALVADOS]

Small cotton town in Suisse-Normande at meeting of two small rivers where Dumont d'Urville, explorer of New Zealand and the Antarctic, was born in 1790 (statue in town hall square). Pontécoulant is a charming little château by a lake (16th to 18th centuries), looking like a family house. Beautifully furnished, with nice English-style gardens. (Shut Monday in winter; Tuesday.)

CORNEVILLE-SUR-RISLE
[EURE]

Poor Corneville (6km SE Pont Audemer) became a national joke around 1900 because of an operetta about it by Planquette. The unfortunate Marquis de la Roche-Thulon generously gave a carillon of twelve bells to be hung in the church, then could not pay for them when they arrived. The innkeeper bought them and put them in the inn. They are still there, in the neo-Gothic Logis now called Les Cloches de Corneville and are played daily except Wednesday.

HOTEL
Les Cloches de Corneville (32.57.01.04): pleasant dining room; nice bedrooms. Regional cooking, reasonable prices. ROOMS C–E. MEALS C–E. Restaurant shut mid-November–mid-December, end February; Wednesday. Hotel open all year.

COURBOYER MANOR
[ORNE]

8km E of Bellême by D920, D9. Delightful, fortified white stone, house with four watchtowers and a massive round tower, all with

conical slate roofs. Built at the end of the 15th century, it is solid
but elegant.

COURSEULLES-SUR-MER
[CALVADOS]

Little seaside resort famous for oysters (brought here from Île
de Ré and St Vaast to mature in beds) and for its west beach
where Winston Churchill landed on 12 June 1944, De Gaulle on
14 June and King George VI on 16 June. It was in the Canadian
sector of Juno Beach. Its little port in the Seulles river mouth
was used until Mulberry harbour had been set up off Arromanches. It is still a fishing harbour but a marina, too. The resort is
growing, is lovely and popular in mid-summer, and is rising as
well as expanding, with holiday apartment blocks. A Sherman
tank recovered from the sea in 1971 stands in the main square.
But oysters are still the main business and a museum about
oyster farming is on the Arromanches road. You can visit the
oyster parks. At Fontaine Henry (6km S) is a château in an
English park – originally mediaeval but beautified with carvings
and lacy stonework after the Renaissance. Inside are fine furniture and paintings. The 13th-century chapel was altered in
Renaissance style. (Complicated opening times – 31.80.00.20).
TOURIST INFORMATION 54 rue Mer (Easter–
September – 31.37.46.80)
MARKET Tuesday, Friday

HOTELS

Crémaillère, boul. de la Plage (31.37.46.73): rooms above the
beach or in a quieter annexe with garden, Le Gytan, ave Com-
battante. Restaurant with sea views. ROOMS B–E. MEALS B–F.
Open all year.
Belle Aurore, 32 rue Foch (31.37.46.23): small modern hotel
opposite little port, with cosy well-equipped bedrooms. Good
meals with excellent fish. ROOMS D–E. MEALS A–E. Shut February; Monday in winter.

COUTAINVILLE
[MANCHE]

Very French *fin-de-siècle* seaside resort with Agon on the Cotentin coast west of Coutances. A charming place, with big sandy beach and dunes and regular French visitors. But it's trying to go modern, with a casino, racecourse, water-skiing, scuba diving, and picturesque old beach huts replaced by straw huts. Agon is really an extension. Across a near wasteland is Pointe d'Agon, with beautiful coastal views.

TOURIST INFORMATION Tourist Office, place 28 Juillet 1944 (15 June–15 September – 33.47.01.46)
MARKETS Tuesday, Thursday, Saturday

HOTELS

Neptune, Promenoir Jersey (33.47.07.66): fine, old, white-painted hotel on promenade, once called 'Grand Hôtel de la Plage'. Comfortable rooms only; bar; no restaurant these days. ROOMS D–E. Shut 1 November–Easter.

Hardy, place 28 Juillet (33.47.04.11): our old favourite. Called Hôtel de la Gare until the station was shut. Hardy family-owned for generations. Emile Hardy has added a few light modern dishes to his delightful classical cooking. Beautiful fresh fish superbly cooked. Some bedrooms small. ROOMS C–F. MEALS A–D plus E (gastronomic). Shut 6 January–7 February; Monday (low season).

COUTANCES
[MANCHE]

A lovely little town on a hilltop crowned by a really beautiful cathedral originally 11th century but rebuilt in the 13th century. Built mostly by the incredible de Hauteville family. Tancred de Hauteville had twelve sons. The sixth Robert Guiscard (1015–85) went to Italy as a warrior, became Duke of Apulia and Calabria, waged constant war against the Saracens and the Byz-

antine Greek Emperors and saved the Pope when Emperor
Henry IV invaded Italy. His brother Roger drove the Saracens
out of Sicily and became Count of Sicily. His son Roger II
became King of Sicily, ruling up to and including Naples, took
the Pope prisoner, took Corfu, plundered Athens, then captured Tripoli, Tunis and Algeria. Coutances cathedral is plain,
but beautifully balanced and has a lovely lantern called Le
Plomb. The central chapel contains a much-venerated 14th-
century statue of Notre-Dame-de-Coutances. Fifteen windows
are 13th century, the oldest show St George, St Thomas (à
Becket) of Canterbury and St Blaise.

Coutances public flower gardens are beautiful, with fine
cedars. They are lit on weekends (1 July–15 September).
Château de Gratot (5km NW) is being restored from its indig-
nity as outbuildings for a farm. Four crumbling towers surround
the old courtyard. For five centuries it belonged to the Argouges
family. In 1439 Jean d'Argouges made himself extremely
unpopular with the French by selling Granville to the English,
enabling them to isolate Mont-St-Michel. Judicious marriages in
the next century brought the family back in favour. Since 1968
volunteers have been restoring the château, which is used for
concerts.

TOURIST INFORMATION Tourist Office, rue Quesnel-
Morinière (33.45.17.79)
MARKET Monday
FESTIVALS around Easter, Jazz Festival

HOTELS

Relais du Viaduct, 25 ave Verdun (33.45.02.68): gastronomic
Relais Routiers. Remarkable value but dearest gastronomic menu
way above Routiers prices. Good chef. Rooms simple, some
noisy. ROOMS A–B. MEALS A–F. Shut 4–27 September.
Tournebride, at Gratot (4km W) (33.45.11.00): simple Norman
auberge with honest regional cooking, good value. MEALS A–D.
Shut 22 December–5 January; Sunday except July, August.

CRÈVE-COEUR-EN-AUGE
[CALVADOS]

The *manoir* is a pretty fortified house surrounded by a large moat, with a 15th-century gatehouse, half-timbered farm, a splendid and remarkable dovecote like a charming little cottage, with nesting niches for 1500 birds, and 12th-century chapel. It is a photogenic ensemble of old Norman country architecture, yet it contains a museum of petroleum! It was restored by Alsatian engineers Conrad and Marcel Schlumberger, who perfected a system of drilling for oil. In the museum are drilling equipment and an audio-visual display explaining oil industry techniques (open daily July, August; afternoons except Wednesday in April, May, June, September; Saturday, Sunday afternoon in March, October, November).

CRIQUEVILLE-EN-AUGE
[CALVADOS]

Tiny hamlet with brick and stone-chequered château of 1584 of three pavilions with huge roofs – very Norman. There are several of these chequered buildings and half-timbered houses in the village, which also has a Commonwealth War Cemetery. Though close to A13 motorway, the village is in pleasant country with views of the coast from the road into Dives-sur-Mer (10km).

CRIEL-PLAGE and MESNIL-VAL
[SEINE-MARITIME]

Two little resorts just south of Le Tréport. Mesnil-Val is the prettier, with a little beach under a cliff and one road of small shops and old houses leading to it. A good hideout with a very charming little hotel, but you do have to watch being stranded by the incoming tide. Both beaches are shingle with sand at low tide.

HOTELS

La Vieille Ferme, Mesnil-Val (35.86.72.18): auberge made from a 17th-century farm, with big flowery garden. Comfortable, not luxurious, bedrooms. Excellent Norman dishes and shellfish served in a fine old dining-room. ROOMS D–E. MEALS C–G. Shut 2–30 January.

CUVERVILLE
[SEINE-MARITIME]

Tiny hamlet of 180 people with a typical little Norman church where the writer André Gide (1859–1951) was married in 1895. In the little churchyard is his grave, marked simply with his name. He lived for some time in the nearby 18th-century château, built by Chevalier de Cuverville, friend and companion of Suffren, French naval hero who fought the English with very mixed results.

DEAUVILLE
[CALVADOS]

Despite jets and changing fashions, Deauville remains one of the greatest international resorts. Its 'season' opens in July and closes on the fourth Sunday in August with the Deauville Grand Prix horse-race. Despite the casino and the fashion parade of the rich, famous and would-be rich and famous along the artificial wooden promenades, Les Planches, the nightly balls and innumerable galas and regattas, the whole great carnival is based on horse-racing. International yearling sales are held in August. During this time hotels, restaurants and the casino are full, branches of Paris's most expensive shops are open, and it is called the '21st Arrondissement of Paris'. At any other time no one with social aspirations would be seen dead there. Then the beautiful, well-dressed women walking 'Les Planches' are not being photographed because they are famous or scandalous but because they are models showing off newly fashionable clothes for the glossy magazines and calendars. But Deauville is no longer empty the rest of the year. New apartments have appeared among the ornate Second Empire and *fin-de-siècle* hotels and villas. There is a 'Port-Grimaud-style' marina at the end of the promenade where boat-owners can tie up their boats outside their cottage doors. The nearby motorway has brought Paris (207km away) close enough to drive to for lunch. Nothing is cheap in Deauville but there are some less pricey hotels.

Deauville only became the fashion centre because Trouville across the river got too greedy. The original casino was built by the owner of Maxims in Paris at the fishing hamlet of Trouville. As it became fashionable Trouville put up the casino rent so high that the Maxim's boss moved across the river and fashionable Paris moved with him. They sent their domestic staff to Trouville!

TOURIST INFORMATION place de la Mairie (closed
Sunday low season – 31.88.21.43)
MARKET Every morning in season; Tuesday rest of year
FESTIVALS July – Bridge festival; August – horse-
racing, yearling sales and polo; September – American
Film Festival; October – Vintage Car Rally Paris-
Deauville

HOTELS

La Nouvelle Résidence, 55 ave République (31.88.07.50): comfortable, reasonably priced; no restaurant. ROOMS C–E. Shut 30 December–1 February.

La Fresnaye, 81 ave République (31.88.09.71): very good value for Deauville; charming, comfortable, period furnishings. No restaurant. ROOMS C–G. Open all year.

La Trophée and Flambée Restaurant, 82 rue Gén Leclerc (31.88.45.86): well-equipped hotel; restaurant serves classic Norman dishes with lots of flaming calvados (and gin!). Very pleasant. ROOMS E, F. MEALS C–F. Open all year.

RESTAURANTS
Ciro's, Promenade des Planches (31.88.18.10): part of Deauville's history. You must try it once at least. Now open for lunch and dinner all the year. Superb cuisine of Christian Girault. MEALS D–G.
Spinnaker, 52 rue Mirabeau (31.88.24.40): bar turned into attractive restaurant with a good young chef. Becoming fashionable. Modernish cooking. MEALS D–G. Shut 25 February–12 March, 16–30 November; Wednesday, Thursday low season.

DEAUX AMANTS HILL
(Côte des Deux Amants)
[SEINE-MARITIME]

On right bank of the Seine, near D19 between Rouen and Les Andelys. Take D20 from Amfreville-sous-les-Monts. This climbs quickly to a hilltop with a fine view over the Seine valley. Follow signposts to Le Plessis and Panorama des Deux Amants. Park. Follow footpath to panorama over the Seine. The name comes from a 12th-century story of two lovers Caliste and Raoul. Caliste's father, the King of Pitrois, would only allow her to marry a man strong enough to carry her at a run to the top of the hill. Raoul made it – then dropped dead. Caliste immediately died of shock. They were buried on the spot.

LA DÉLIVERANDE
[CALVADOS]

3km from Langrune-sur-Mer, west of Ouistreham is the twin-spired Basilica of Our Lady of Déliverande, mid-19th-century neo-Gothic, but containing a highly venerated Black Madonna, unearthed by sheep. Pilgrimages are on feast days to the Virgin (15 August and 8 September) and the local feast day on the Thursday after 15th August.

DIÉLETTE
[MANCHE]

Tiny port on the west Cotentin coast used for centuries as a refuge by fishermen and small boats – the only one between Carteret and Goury on the tip of the Cherbourg Peninsula. A long breakwater protects the small harbour. At low tide there is a sandy beach. This is a coast of sandy bays and hamlets still little discovered by tourists, with a few inland villages. 3km S is the 17th-century château of Flamanville in classical Louis XIV style with a park in which, thanks to the warming Gulf Stream hitting this Carteret coast, palm trees are reflected in a lake. Flamanville has a new neighbour – a nuclear station built into the rocks.

DIEPPE
[see Major Towns, page 23]

DIVES-SUR-MER
[see Cabourg, page 99]

DOMFRONT
[ORNE]

Of the historic castle of Domfront, high above the valley of the Varenne, all that remains are two massive sections of the keep, surrounded by flower gardens. But many of its 24 rampart towers remain. It saw some violent days and played its part in the histories of England and France before it was dismantled by order of Henri IV in the 17th century.

Old half-timbered houses still remain in the narrow streets and on the river bank below, a beautiful little Romanesque

church where Thomas à Becket said Mass has survived foreshor-
tening to build a road last century. Standing on its rocky ridge
above orchards of pears, Domfront is very attractive in spring
and summer, though its concrete neo-Byzantine church of St
Julien built in 1924 is ugly.

The bellicose Bellême family (the Montgomerys) built the
castle in 1011, but the local people revolted against them and
petitioned for the protection of Henri Beauclerc, third son of
William the Conqueror. When he became King of England in
1100, Domfront became English. Henry II of England and his
wife Eleanor held court here with poets and troubadours and
here Henry learned from the Vatican that his penance for
Thomas à Becket's murder was to walk bare-footed to Canterbury to be scourged by monks. The English and French fought
over the castle throughout the Hundred Years War. The English left in 1450.

A Montgomery who had killed Henri II (of France) withstood
the bloodiest siege of the castle. In 1559 Captain Gabriel de
Montgomery of the Scots Guards, then fighting for the French
against England, accidentally killed the French king in a jousting
match, thus making Catherine de Médicis a widow and robbing
Diane de Poitiers of her lover. Montgomery converted to Calvin-
ism and became a Protestant leader. He then held Domfront
castle with 150 men against a Royalist Catholic French Army but
wounds, illness and starvation reduced his force to fifteen sick
men, and he surrendered on a promise that lives would be
spared. Catherine broke her promise, had him stripped of his
honours and executed.

In Domfront's town-hall museum is a room of drawings and
paintings of the local artist Charles Léandre (1862–1934) who
painted the countryside and its people but, unlike Millet,
showed the tougher, bitter side of country life.

TOURIST INFORMATION rue Fossés-Plissons
(33.38.53.27)

FESTIVAL July – International Folklore

HOTELS
Poste, 25 rue Maréchal-Foch (33.38.51.00): Relais Gastronomi-

que; modern Logis. Pleasant atmosphere. Pure Norman dishes –
pear cider (*célèbre poiré*). Comfortable lounge. ROOMS A–D.
MEALS A–F. Shut 25 January–end February; Sunday evening,
Monday in winter.

France, rue Mont-St-Michel (33.38.51.44): traditional auberge,
garden, tennis, private fishing. Meals remarkable value. Norman farmhouse cooking. ROOMS B–D. MEALS A–D. Shut 6
January–13 February; restaurant shut Monday evening, Tuesday except 15 June–15 September.

DONVILLE-LES-BAINS
[MANCHE]

One of the family resorts with sandy beaches N of Granville on
west coast of Cotentin peninsula. Others are Bréville,
Coudeville, St Martin-de-Bréhal.

DUCEY
[MANCHE]

Between Ducey and St Hilaire-du-Harcouët at the bottom of the
Cotentin peninsula, the Sélune river has been dammed to form
two long lakes – Lac de la Roche qui Boit and Lac du Vezins,
very popular for fishing and sailing. There is no road round
them, but you can follow the little roads D78 from Ducey over
the Vezins bridge or D582 off N176 Ducey–St Hilaire road to
reach them. Ducey itself is famed for salmon fishing.

HOTELS

Auberge de la Sélune, 2 rue St Germain (33.48.53.62): garden to
the river. Jean-Pierre Girras is a very good cook. Good value.
ROOMS C–D. MEALS A–D. Shut 20 January–20 February; Monday in winter.

DUCLAIR
[Seine-Maritime]

Not many tourists find this pleasant Seine-side town on the
north bank. It is at the top of a huge loop of the snaking river,
between Caudebec and Rouen. Its quay with bars, benches and
shady lime trees is a good place to watch the passing barges and
ships on the river. A *bac* (ferry) crosses the river to yacht moor-
ings. Alas, some lorries have discovered this ferry and there can
be queues. A little road on the other bank crosses the river loop,
then follows the bank as far as the delightful village of La Bouille
(page 92). Another riverside road on the north bank follows the
Jumièges loop where, from mid-April to mid-May, the apple
blossom astounds even men of Kent.

   St Denis Church, with a 12th-century belfry crowned with a
16th-century spire, has treasures from the nearby old Jumièges
abbey, including eleven large stone figures of the apostles. Most
of the stained glass is 16th-century, with one modern *Pentecoste*
by Max Ingrand (1908–69), who also helped with the church's
restoration.

Tourist Information Hôtel de Ville (35.37.50.06).

Market Tuesday

HOTELS

Poste, 286 Quai Libération (35.37.50.04): on the Seine quayside.
Known inevitably for Rouen duckling. Rooms B. Meals A–E.
Shut 1–15 July; part November and February; Sunday evening;
restaurant on Mondays.

Parc, 721 ave Président-Coty (35.37.50.31): beside the Seine in a
fin-de-siècle mansion with fine garden. Honest, excellent, old-
fashioned Norman dishes. Lovely! Book. Meals D–E. Shut 20
December–20 January; Sunday evening, Monday.

EAWY FOREST
[SEINE-MARITIME]

Beautiful beech woodlands of 6600 hectares bordered by the Varenne and Béthune rivers SE of Dieppe, with lovely walks and drives on small forest drives and roads. Allée des Limousins, which cuts straight through crossing beautiful shaded valleys, is a fire break twenty metres wide and 14km long. Picnic spots and marked trails help the French enjoy their forests. Two of the most attractive drives across it are Pommereval on D915 to near Bellencombe and to St Saëns. Another peaceful route is to take D22 from Les Grandes Ventes on D915, turn left on D154, then follow signs left to Carrefour de la Heuze, near a pilgrim chapel dedicated to the patron saint of travellers, St Christopher. The forest is rich in hamlets, manor houses and little churches.

ECAQUELON
[EURE]

Hamlet beautifully situated in deep woodland of Montfort forest, east of Montfort-sur-Risle. Its church contains very fine 16th-century wood carvings and a 15th-century alabaster altar-piece from England.

ECOUIS
(EURE)

A beautiful narrow road NE from Les Andelys runs 8km to this village in the Vexin, dominated by the twin towers of its 14th-century collegiate church. The church is rather sad-looking but has become an interesting museum of 14th to 17th century religious sculpture. Some beautiful works of art, including a 14th-century chalice of Jean de Marigny, who built the church, are shut in a first floor room but you can see them by applying to the curé.

The most famous and beautiful statue, now known as Our Lady of Écouis, was long called St Mary the Egyptian. She is a ravishingly lovely, sinuous lady with flowing draperies. The statue of St Agnes, with long rippling hair, is ravishing, too. The choir stalls by a local Norman artist, show a fine Renaissance influence.

ÉCOUVES FOREST
[ORNE]

How beautifully the French keep their national forests and how well they provide for recreation within them. Where others put up barriers, they provide marked paths for walkers. Only the private forests forbid you to enter.

Écouves Forest covers 14,973 hectares of superb oak, beech, Norman pine and spruce on the eastward hills of Lower Normandy, rising as high as 417 metres at the Signal d'Écouves (Écouves Beacon), joint highest point in Western France. Deer and boar roam wild. The forest stretches from near Sées in the north to within 10km of Alençon. Take D908 from Sées onto D226. At Carrefour de la Croix de Médavy stands a tank-memorial to the defeat of German Panzers in 1944 by General Leclerc's Free French 2nd Division from Britain, which freed Alençon on 18 August 1944. A forest road leads to Carrefour Croix-Madame, crossroads, marked by an ancient milestone and lovely pine trees. D204 left with nice views leads to D26. Turn right on a forest road and park. A long walk (nearly an hour) takes you to Vignage rocks with lovely forest views. On the edge of the forest is another memorial to the 2nd Armoured Division. D26 leads to Alençon.

ELBEUF
[SEINE-MARITIME]

Industrial town on the Seine, east of Rouen. Once a major textile town, now chemical, engineering and metallurgical industries, plus a Renault engine factory. André Maurois (1885–1967), author of *The Silences of Colonel Bramble* (a novel based on his experiences as a liaison officer with the British in the trenches in the 1914–18 War), *Ariel* (brilliant life of Shelley) and biographies of Proust, Disraeli, Voltaire and Sir Alexander Fleming (discoverer of penicillin) was born in Elbeuf and lived here thirty years, but no one seems to care much. The Flamboyant church of St Étienne has 16th-century stained glass windows and the windows of the Gothic church of St John date from 1500.

TOURIST INFORMATION 28 rue Henry (35.77.03.78)
MARKETS Tuesday, Thursday, Saturday morning

RESTAURANT WITH ROOMS
Naudin, 1 rue Mar.-Gallieni (35.77.06.94): in old quarter; where locals lunch. Old-style, simple dishes well-cooked, bistro-style. 4 simple rooms. ROOMS A–B. MEALS C–E. Shut 1–28 August; Saturday evening, Sunday evening.

ÉPRON
[CALVADOS]

On D7 north from Caen. Wiped out in 1944. Rebuilt, on proceeds of collection of old banknotes made by French radio.

ÉTRETAT
[SEINE-MARITIME]

Étretat is one of those delightful holiday resorts which succeeds in absorbing changing fashions, keeping young and lively (in summer, certainly) yet remaining itself. The light and grandeur of its setting between cliffs eroded into fantastic shapes drew painters and romantics to it when it was a fishing village last century. Victor Hugo thought everything about it was admirable. Maupassant lived in Étretat and his mentor Flaubert was a regular visitor, so was Gide. Boudin, Courbet, Dégas and Matisse all came to paint the cliffs. Offenbach had a house there and his son-in-law became Mayor. But it was the Parisian writer Alphonse Karr, novelist and editor of *Le Figaro*, who discovered the little village in 1833, adopted it, and made it fashionable with Parisians. It remained so until the 1914–18 War, after which its rival Deauville took over. The English came to Étretat mostly for golf, staying in the Dormy Golf Hotel. Hitler's Todt organisation took over after the German Occupation in 1940, knocking down lovely villas and fortifying it as part of the West Wall against Allied invasion. Napoleon had previously intended to fortify it against the English. But Étretat has recovered. Parisians can drive down easily for weekends. Many own flats or studios in converted villas or in new blocks. From spring to autumn, the Casino is lively with pop music, the promenade and beach lively with people. Étretat sleeps in winter, when many hotels close.

The covered market has been rebuilt in original style opposite the Casino in place Maréchal-Foch.

In the nave of Notre Dame church, once a dependence of the great abbey of Fécamp, are pillars with 11th-century Romanesque geometric designs. Traditional thatched fisherman's huts reconstructed on the beach now sell shellfish.

The natural arches and needles cut by the sea in the soft Caux cliffs are the true attraction. A solitary needle rock 700 metres high stands in the water. The northern cliff, Falaise d'Amont, is topped by the slender spire of Notre-Dame-de-la-Garde Chapel. You can drive this far, but most people climb the steps and path. There are benches if you need to rest. By the chapel is a museum dedicated to the two French aviators, Charles Nungesser and François Coli, killed in a attempt to cross the North Atlantic in 1927. The view from the chapel over Étretat and the cliffs is splendid but you can see even more of the coast by taking the path to the belvedere at the end of the cliff.

Cliffs at Étretat

To reach Falaise d'Aval at the other end of Étretat, climb wooden steps from the promenade and follow a path. At the crest, directly above the Porte d'Aval arch, is a German gun emplacement from which there is a superb view. By skirting the golf-course it's about a half-hour walk to Cap d'Antifer (*see* Bruneval page 98).

TOURIST INFORMATION Tourist Office, Hôtel-de-Ville
(15 June–15 September – 35.27.05.21)

HOTELS

Dormy House, route du Havre (35.27.07.88): on cliff, fine views, garden, peaceful; largely a golf hotel. ROOMS D–F. MEALS D–E. Shut mid-November–25 March.

Welcome, 10 ave Verdun (35.27.00.89): well-named; friendly. Good for families. ROOMS C–D. MEALS B–F. Shut February; Wednesday.

Donjon, chemin St Clair (35.27.08.23): very comfortable rooms in old part overlooking rocks. Good setting for Agatha Christie story. Garden, pool. Half-pension only F–G. Meals E-G. Shut 15 November–15 December, early January–mid-February.

RESTAURANT
Roches Blanches, terrasse Eugène-Boudin (35.27.07.34): good value restaurant. MEALS A–D. Shut October, 5 January–5 February; Wednesday; Tuesday and Thursday low season.

EU
[SEINE-MARITIME]

Eu is a drowsy little town, except when summer traffic pours through on the way to the resort of Le Tréport 5km away. It is situated between Eu forest and the sea. The vast castle, beloved by King Louis-Philippe and his friend Queen Victoria, who stayed there as his guest, was begun in 1578 by Henri, Duc de Guise, the notorious assassin of the St Bartholomew's Day massacre of Protestants, and leader of the extremist Catholic League. He himself was assassinated by Henri III for plotting to become king. So the present castle is only part of his plan. It has been restored often since, and not improved. It was the favourite residence of Louis-Philippe, who reigned from 1830–1848 and that made the whole area fashionable, including Tréport. Inside it is beautifully furnished, with many of Louis-Philippe's possessions which he left behind when he fled to exile at Claremont in Surrey – some fine portraits, tapestries, wall-hangings and glass. His grandson, the Count of Paris, hired Viollet-le-Duc, rebuilder of Notre Dame in Paris, to redecorate it between 1872 and 1879. It now houses the Hôtel de Ville.

Eu was burned down in 1475 by Louis XI to stop the English taking it. Its castle was destroyed. In the little chapel which still exists, William, sixth Duke of Normandy, married his cousin Matilda in 1050. He became William the Conqueror.

The 12th to 13th century collegiate church of Eu, Notre Dame et St Laurent, is dedicated to an Irish saint, St Lawrence

O'Toole, Primate of Ireland, who died in Eu in 1181. It was restored by Viollet-le-Duc. The outside is a mass of turreted and pinnacled buttresses. The inside is huge and harmonious. Louis-Philippe restored the crypt in 1828. In it are tombs of the Counts of Eu (Artois family) and a recumbent statue of the Irish saint. The historic church organ was repaired in 1977 and the greatest organists in France play it.

The forest of Eu lies between the rivers Bresle and Yères, with glades of huge beeches crossed by little roads and paths, but with big patches of open space and a few hamlets. It covers 9395 hectares.

TOURIST INFORMATION Tourist Office, 41 rue Bignon
(35.86.04.68)
MARKET Friday morning

HOTELS
Pavillon Joinville, route de Tréport (35.86.24.03): old hunting lodge of Louis-Philippe's son, Duc de Joinville, later a hideout of a Duke of Westminster. Relais du Silence with true 'calm, tranquillity and repose'. Fine, old rooms with big, oak doors behind which you hear nothing. In a park with gardens and pastures of grazing horses. Swimming pool. Restaurant in the grounds 'La Ferme Modèle'. ROOMS F–G. MEALS C–F. Open all year.
Relais, 1 place Albert 1er (35.86.14.88): quiet rooms; good value meals. ROOMS B–D. MEALS A–D. Shut 31 August–18 September; 31 January–14 February. Restaurant shut Sunday evening, Monday.

EVREUX
[EURE]

Through centuries, Evreux on the river Iton has been burned down by English and French kings, German and Allied air forces. Each time it has risen from the ashes, including its Notre Dame cathedral. First burned down in 1119 by England's Henry I, it has been rebuilt or largely repaired several times, though it once stood derelict for two centuries. The upper parts were badly damaged in 1940 when Evreux burned for a week after a German air raid. It is a formidable building in 12th to 17th-century styles which blend surprisingly well. Its main treasures are its stained glass, going back to the 14th century, and its carved wood screens. The glass was removed in 1939 for safe keeping. The 15th-century windows in the Lady Chapel show the lords of France at the coronation of Louis XI. The old abbey church St Taurinus (14th to 15th century) has a beautiful 13th-century reliquary of gilt, silver and enamel given by Louis XI. In the form of a miniature chapel, it is one of the best works of silversmith's art in France. The 15th-century Flamboyant Bishop's Palace houses an archaeological museum with a room of fine paintings including Impressionists (shut Mondays, part November).

Evreux, still a prosperous market town, has been rebuilt as a modern city while preserving as many as possible of its old monuments. Its avenues and squares are tree-lined, softening the modernity. You can walk along the old ramparts beside the river, a tributary of the Eure, which has been cleaned up and canalised between old stone walls. Beside it is the Tour de l'Horloge, an elegant 15th-century belfry tower which survived all the destruction. The public flower gardens are beautiful.

TOURIST INFORMATION Tourist Office, 35 rue Dr Oursel (32.38.21.61)

HOTELS

Normandy, 37 rue Edouard-Feray (32.33.14.40): old Norman style; comfortable; classic cooking. ROOMS E. MEALS A–F. Restaurant shut August; Sunday.

France, 29 rue St Thomas (32.39.09.25): good, modern dishes served in elegant surroundings. Pricey meals. Rooms comfortable, fairly simple. ROOMS B–D. MEALS E–G. Restaurant shut Sunday evening, Monday.

RESTAURANTS

Auberge de Parville, at Parville, 3km W by N13 (32.39.36.63): charming, away from traffic; lovely Norman house; classic regional cooking with modern touches. MEALS C–F. Shut Monday; Sunday and Wednesday evenings.

FALAISE
[CALVADOS]

You would not believe that it ever happened. Falaise today is a neat market town, with space around its new buildings which are mellowing already. It is prosperous and happy. Its magnificent castle stands guard and the whole town is splendidly floodlit on summer's evenings. But the name of Falaise rang through the world in August 1944 as the Germans used it as a centre for their last stand in Normandy in the bocage country around it. Poor, peaceful little Falaise was horribly mutilated in the fighting. Even its 13th-century Talbot tower was used as a gunpost as machine guns were fired through its windows. Happily the old west quarter escaped damage and in the centre is a large statue of Falaise's most famous son. On horseback, flanked by the first six Dukes of Normandy, sits William the Conqueror, born in the château on the escarpment above the town. The cobbled square is correctly called Place Guillaume-le-Conquérant. A steep slope from the square leads to the remains of the castle. The windows

Statue of William the Conqueror, Falaise

of the Great Hall are from the 11th century. The dungeon is open to visitors (shut in October, Tuesdays and Sundays also in winter). Among those imprisoned here were Arthur, nephew of King John of England, and King William 'The Lion of Scotland', after an argument with the English King. In St Poix chapel is a memorial to 315 of William's companions at the battle of Hastings – and the names remind Britons of their ancestry.

The story of William's birth is one of great romance. Returning from a hunt, Robert, seventeen-year-old younger son of Richard II, Duke of Normandy, fell for a young girl washing clothes in a stream, her skirts held provocatively high. She was Arlette, daughter of a rich tanner. He spied on her from the castle and let it be known secretly that he desired her. Arlette's father told her that she must do as she wished. Scorning furtive visits to the castle, she put on her finery and rode proudly through the main gates. She bore a son, called William, and stayed at the castle to bring him up.

In 1159 Henry II of England and his wife Eleanor of Aquitaine held a Court of Love within the walls. Troubadours came from all over Europe – the first Pop Concert!

By the river Ante, next to the swimming pool, is Fontaine d'Arlette where Robert spotted the girl. The view from here to the château is impressive. Trinité church, further along the river by a lake, is worth visiting. The west end is Gothic, the east has ornate Renaissance flying buttresses.

Falaise is an attractive centre for exploring the Suisse-Normande. Even a few kilometres away are some interesting and attractive places.

Aubigny, a hamlet 4km N along N158 has a fine 16th-century castle and in its church six interesting statues of the lords of Aubigny dressed in the clothes of their time.

Brèche au Diable, further north, is a gorge hollowed out of the limestone by the Laizon river. A steep path leads down it. At the top beside a spinney is a florid tomb to the 18th-century actress Marie Joly, with tearful lines by her husband. The gorge is just off D261. Another 4km along this road is Assy château, a superb 18th-century manor with an elegant portico of Corinthian columns. It is a near-perfect Classical house. Its elegance is enhanced by a beautiful avenue to the door.

TOURIST INFORMATION Falaise Tourist Office, 32 rue
Georges-Clémenceau (31.90.17.26)

HOTELS

Normandie, 4 rue Amiral-Courbet (31.90.18.26): modern unin-
teresting building but reasonable rooms. Excellent value cheap
menus. Useful. ROOMS B–C. MEALS A–C. Restaurant shut
Sunday.
Poste, 38 rue Georges-Clémenceau (31.90.13.14): noisy street for
overnight but excellent bargain meals of Norman dishes.
ROOMS B–C. MEALS A–F. Shut third week October, 20
December–15 January; restaurant shut Sunday evening,
Monday.

RESTAURANT

L'Attaché, on N158 (31.90.05.38): very good rustic restaurant for
solid classical meals with good meat. Used by locals. Bargain
cheap menus. MEALS A–C. Shut Tuesday, Wednesday evenings.

FÉCAMP
[SEINE-MARITIME]

An abbey, Bénédictine liqueur, Guy de Maupassant and cod
made Fécamp prosperous and renowned. Its big trawlers fished
for cod as far as the Newfoundland Banks and coastal trawlers
brought in mackerel and herring. Industry depended on
fishing, canning plants, fertiliser production, net and rope
manufacture and cod drying for the old French national dish of
Aïoli – dried cod with garlic mayonnaise. In the last few years the
long-distance fishing fleet has gone the way of the Arctic fleets of
Hull and Grimsby. Mixed cargoes land on the quays, especially
of wood from Scandinavia and sand for glass production. Fishing has switched to quality fish – sole, turbot, sea-bass with some
cod from Iceland for drying. And they smoke salmon, imported
from Ireland, Iceland and Norway. The outer harbour is a
pleasure yacht marina with a scuba-diving centre, but the beach
is rather dull, though Fécamp remains a family resort.

There was a monastery in Fécamp from the 7th century. Legend has it that a mysterious boat came ashore in the 1st century with a few drops of Christ's blood in a lead container and the monastery grew later to shelter it. Duke Richard I built La Trinité Abbey Church and his son, Richard II, founded a new Benedictine Abbey, persuading the monks of Dijon to move in 1003 to Fécamp. Until Mont-St-Michel was built, Fécamp was the main pilgrimage centre of Normandy and the abbots used troubadours and minstrels as publicists to spread its fame. It became powerful and rich. 'Gold, silver and silken ornaments shine everywhere,' reported one bishop.

Richard's church was struck by lightning and it was rebuilt in the 12th to 13th centuries and much altered in the 15th and 18th centuries. Today it is something of a hotch-potch of styles, but dignified. It still houses the precious relic of blood, and pilgrims fill the church on the Tuesday and Thursday after Trinity Sunday. It is very large and dominating, longer than Notre Dame in Paris, and contains fine carvings and interesting statues, including a splendid group *Death of the Virgin*.

An 18th-century house is the municipal museum, with 16th-century marine paintings, a good 19th-century landscape by Diaz (Barbizon school – 1807–76) and sketches by Eugène Delacroix, the Romantic painter, and Monet.

The extraordinary 19th-century Benedictine château which houses a very varied museum with fine furniture, is part of the liqueur distillery buildings (*see* Drink page 15). The ruins of the 12th-century Valmont Abbey are 11km E. Only the Renaissance choir remains of the old Abbey Church but the charming Lady Chapel has remained intact. (Closed Wednesdays, Sundays except in school holidays.) The nearby castle, property of the Sires d'Estouville, still has its square keep built in the time of William the Conqueror, and a Renaissance residence still lived in. Victor Hugo wrote of it in *Notre Dame de Paris*.

TOURIST INFORMATION Tourist Office, place Bellet
(35.28.20.51)
MARKET Saturday – large market last Saturday each
month

HOTELS

Angleterre, 83 rue Plage (35.28.01.60): by the sea; well run. ROOMS B–E. MEALS A–E. Open all year.

Auberge de la Rouge, 2km S by D940 at St Léonard (35.28.07.59): old posting inn; eight rooms open onto a little garden. Norman meals, recently modernised, still very good. ROOMS D–E. MEALS B (weekdays), E–G. Restaurant shut Sunday evening, Monday.

RESTAURANTS

Escalier, 101 Quai Bérigny (35.28.26.79): very good value; fresh local fish; Norman dishes. MEALS B–D. Shut 25 October–6 November; Sunday evening, Monday out of season.

Viking, 63 boul. Albert I (35.29.22.92): on sea front; good quality, portions and service. MEALS B–F. Shut Monday.

Martin, 18 place St Étienne, behind post office (35.28.23.82): Norman décor; cheap, excellent value; simple Norman dishes (cod or sole in cider; moules marinières). MEALS A–D. Shut 1–19 March, 1–18 September; Sunday evening, Monday.

LA FERRIÈRE-SUR-RISLE
[EURE]

A pretty road running between Beaumont-le-Roger and the Conches forest crosses the river Risle valley at La Ferrière, a photogenic village with a 13th to 14th-century church with unusual statues of the Virgin and Child, St Anne and St Michael. 14th-century market place. Leisure centre 2km away with pony rides, mini-golf, archery, shooting range, etc, refreshments (April–September).

HOTEL

Croissant (32.30.70.13): old, picturesque inn, simple bedrooms; good value meals. ROOMS A–C. MEALS A–C. Shut 1–8 October, 10 January–10 February; Sunday evening, Monday.

LA FERTÉ
[SEINE-MARITIME]

On a hill just off D921 S of Forges-les-Eaux, the village marks the beginning of the strange Bray 'boutonière' (button-hole) cut into the hills by the Andelle river and its tributaries. You can see this clear-cut Bray depression like a huge bowl across the countryside.

LA FERTÉ-MACÉ
[ORNE]

Small town near Bagnoles-de-l'Orne with a large market, but mainly industrial. It is known for tripe cooked on skewers. The church, with an ornate façade, is modern but retains its 11th-century Romanesque tower and a carillon of sixteen bells. Some old streets are still cobbled, and partly pedestrianised.

TOURIST INFORMATION Tourist Office, 13 rue Victoire
(33.37.10.97)
MARKET Thursday
FESTIVAL March – Festival of Tripe

HOTELS

Nouvel et Restaurant Le Céleste, 6 rue Victoire (33.37.22.33): The chef has taken over the hotel. Meals are excellent value. The place to try local tripe or other Norman dishes. ROOMS A–C. MEALS A–F. Shut January, October; Sunday evening, Monday.
Clouet, Le Clouet (33.37.18.22): bright, comfortable, flowery terrace; good value. ROOMS C–D. MEALS A–G. Shut January; Sunday evening, Monday in winter.

FILIÈRES CHÂTEAU
[SEINE-MARITIME]

At Gommerville off N15 from Le Havre to Bolbec. An avenue leads to the main courtyard, which is surrounded by a moat. Built between the 16th and 18th centuries in Caen limestone by the Mirivilles family whose descendants own it. The two styles of architecture do not quite blend, but the internal decorations are impressive. Collections include Oriental porcelain and wall-hangings, Sèvres medallions, fine furniture, an excellent portrait of Louis XV by Van Loo, and Fragonard lithographs (open Wednesdays, Saturdays, Sundays from Easter–All Saints' Day). The park was laid out in the 17th century by Le Nôtre who designed Versailles gardens.

FLERS
[ORNE]

Industrial town, formerly cotton mills, now making electro-mechanical equipment. It was rebuilt after 1944 war damage. The 16th to 18th century château has towers reflected in its moat. It now contains the town hall, library and museum, which has paintings by artists of the 19th-century Barbizon school (Corot, Diaz, Daubigny) and pre-Impressionists (Boudin, Lepine) and ceramics by Jean Cocteau. Also paintings of bocage peasant life by local artists, such as Charles Léandre (open Easter–October).

TOURIST INFORMATION 1 place de Gaulle
(33.65.06.75)
MARKET Wednesday

RESTAURANT
Relais Fleuri, 115 rue Schnetz (33.65.23.89): fine old-fashioned French cooking. Mme Ledezert has been here forty years. Nouvelle enthusiasts keep away! Old Norman décor with ver-

anda to garden. CARTE only D–G. Shut 23 July–23 August;
Saturday evening, Sunday.

FONTAINE-L'ABBÉ
[EURE]

Very attractive, very Norman village in the Charentonne valley.
Louis XIII château.

FORGES-LES-EAUX
[SEINE-MARITIME]

Restful small spa 55km from Dieppe by D915 and 42km from
Rouen in the green 'buttonhole' of Bray Region. Lovely park
and sailing lake. Four rivers start here and eight curative waters
can be drunk in the buvette below the white casino. In the park
is the grotto where Louis XIII and his Queen, Anne of Austria,
and Richelieu drank the waters. Louis and Richelieu are still
there – in enormous bronze statues. Voltaire said that the water
contained more vitriol than ink – even from his pen. Near the
park gates are two richly-decorated façades of very different
origins. The nearest to the Casino came from Louis XV's hunting lodge near Versailles and the other 17th-century façade was
once part of a Carmelite Convent at Gisors. Forges is fairly quiet
but its Casino kept it busy for many years after 1919 when they
were banned within 100km of Paris. Forges is 116km away.

TOURIST INFORMATION Tourist Office in Hôtel de
Ville grounds (35.90.52.10)
MARKET Thursday
FESTIVAL July – horse fair

RESTAURANT WITH ROOMS
Paix, 17 rue Neufchatel (35.90.51.22): simple rooms; some of
the best value meals in Normandy. Regional cooking by Rémy

Michel of fresh local food. ROOMS A–B. MEALS A–C. Shut 15
December–15 January; Sunday evening, Monday low season.

Beau Lieu, route Gournay-en-Bray 2km (35.90.50.36): Patrick
Ramelet, taught by André Jeunet at Arbois, has restored an old
farm into a lovely dining room with excellent food. MEALS C–F.
Shut 16–27 January, part February; Monday and Tuesday and
Wednesday evenings low season.

FRESNAY-SUR-SARTHE
[SARTHE]

Attractive village on a rocky height above the Sarthe river, with
good fishing. Just over the Sarthe border from Orne. A pleasant
centre for exploring the Mancelle Alps, it has a 12th-century
church with an unusual octagonal belfry, and lovely 16th-
century carved oak doors showing Christ crucified, the Apostles
and the Virgin. In a tower of the castle ruin is an exhibition of
headdresses of different parts of France (open daily July,
August; Sundays April–September).

TOURIST INFORMATION Syndicat d'Initiative, place
Bassum (43.34.88.04 in season)

HOTEL
Ronsin, 5 ave Charles de Gaulle (43.97.20.10): Logis de France.
ROOMS B–D. MEALS A–D. Shut Sunday evening, Monday lunch
from 15 September–15 June.

GACÉ
[ORNE]

Not very interesting but has a useful Saturday afternoon market
and a good overnight hotel.

HOTEL

Castel Morphée, 2 rue Lisieux (33.35.51.01): 19th century typical Norman bourgeois house in a garden. Charming bedrooms. No restaurant. ROOMS D–E. Shut January, February.

GAILLON
[EURE]

Property of the Archbishops of Rouen since the reign of Philippe-Auguste, it was the site of the first great Renaissance building in France. Returning from an expedition to Italy with Louis XII at the end of the 15th century, Georges d'Amboise, the Archbishop, knocked down Gaillon château and built a magnificent palace. It was wrecked in the Revolution. The beautiful entrance lodge, flanked by two towers, remains. But the Beaux Arts department are restoring the château to house the Museum of Upper Normandy.

GENÊTS
[MANCHE]

This tiny resort has a formidable granite church with a wooden roof (12th to 14th century) and sands stretching across the bay to Mont-St-Michel. An annual pilgrimage across the bay takes place in July, but do not attempt to walk across without a guide or you could sink in quicksands (apply at Maison de la Baie 33.70.83.42).

GISORS
[EURE]

The great castle standing over the town was built in 1096 by Robert de Bellême, Earl of Shrewsbury, for William Rufus, King of England and Duke of Normandy, on the frontier of Normandy and France. Today it contrasts strangely with the friendly little tourist town astride the river Epte. It was so important for Normandy's defence that Henry I of England made it virtually impregnable, almost as strong as Richard Coeur-de-Lion's castle at Les Andelys. It never fell by assault but King John surrendered it to King Philippe-Auguste of France, and he strengthened it further by building a huge surrounding wall and enlarging the keep. It changed hands between French and English by treaty several times. The 11th-century circular keep stands on a mound flanked by a watch tower. It was originally surrounded by a moat, replaced now by pretty tree-lined gardens which soften its military threat. Biggest of the eight towers, the three-storey prisoners' tower added by Philippe-Auguste in the 12th century, has a pointed, arched chamber with chimney, ovens and a well built into its massive walls. In the dungeon below is graffiti showing dancing and tournaments, and religious scenes from the 15th and 16th centuries. (Castle closed 15 December–1 February.)

From the ramparts are fine views. You can see the imposing Church of St Gervais and St Protais, built over many centuries. The chancel (1249) is most interesting. Much is Gothic but the west façade is Renaissance and has a delicate carved doorway with two towers.

Though heavily bombed in 1940 Gisors has kept its character. The Guild of Tanners on a river bend has a timbered 17th-century wash-house.

TOURIST INFORMATION 1 place Carmélites
(32.55.20.28)
MARKETS Monday, Friday, Sunday

HOTELS

Moderne, place Gare (32.55.23.51): Logis. Classical cooking. Cheap. ROOMS B–E. MEALS A–C. Restaurant shut 13 July–10 August; 20 December–10 January; Sunday evening, Monday.
Trois Poissons, 13 rue Cappeville (32.55.01.09): interesting cooking from old Norman to inventive; good fish. Excellent value. ROOMS (simple) A–B. MEALS A–E. Hotel shut 1 October–30

March. Restaurant shut Christmas, New Year; 9–30 June. Both shut Monday evening, Tuesday.

Dieppe, 1 ave de la Gare (32.55.25.54): real Norman cuisine; good value. ROOMS B. MEALS A–C. Shut mid-June to mid-July; Thursday evening, Friday.

Château de la Rapée, at Bazincourt-sur-Epte, 4km N of Gisors by D14 (32.55.11.61): quiet turreted manor in countryside by a forest. Spacious, well-equipped bedrooms. Mostly antique furniture; good old-style Norman cooking. ROOMS E–F. MEALS D–E. Shut mid-August to 1 September; 12 January–1 March; Tuesday in winter, Wednesday.

GIVERNY
[EURE]

Claude Monet, most dedicated of the Impressionist painters, lived in this hamlet SE of Vernon from 1883 until his death in

Gardens at Giverny

1926. In a peaceful setting of poplars and willows, his long, low, pink-and-green house overlooks the valley of the Epte. The colourful gardens have been restored and replanted with powerful displays of flowers, using the same types of roses and herbaceous plants that were known in his day. The water-garden with its lily pond and Japanese bridge is bigger and even more impressive than it seems from his many paintings. The visit to both house and garden are fascinating (closed Monday). Of all the Impressionist artists, Monet kept most closely to its ideas of the effects of changing light on scenes. The word Impressionist came from his painting *Impression – Sunrise*. He painted his lily pond again and again, in mist, sunshine and at sunset, with the lilies in bud or full bloom. Despite many summer visitors, the garden still has an air of nostalgia, as if it was only yesterday that the nearly blind old man of eight-six looked at his lilies for the last time.

GOURNAY-EN-BRAY
[SEINE-MARITIME]

Still the centre of a big cheese industry in the rich dairy pastures of Bray, it started to become prosperous in 1850 when a farmer's wife and her Swiss cowherd mixed cream with unbroken curds and invented Petit-Suisse cheese, soft, unsalted and sold in tiny cylinders. Though the cheese is made now in many places, Gournay makes most. It is on the edge of Forêt de Lyons, with superb beeches and charming hamlets. Take the N30 11km northwards, then a local road, to reach Gerberoy, a fortified hilltop town over the border in Oise. It was almost abandoned from the 17th century until the modern painter Le Sidaner (1862–1939) and his friends restored it and moved there.

TOURIST INFORMATION (Gournay) Syndicat
d'Initiative, 4 porte de Paris (35.90.28.34)
MARKETS Tuesday, Friday, Sunday

GOURY
[MANCHE]

Tiny harbour on Cap de la Hague west of Cherbourg which is the only refuge for fishing boats and yachts from the notorious current of the Alderney Race. The lifeboat has saved countless lives.

GRANDCAMP-MAISY
[CALVADOS]

Fishing port and yacht harbour on the wartime Omaha beach sector east of Isigny; much rebuilt after damage in 1944 when liberated by American troops. Interesting to anyone who likes small boats or superb fish. Blackboards on the quayside tell you when fishing boats are due to dock and what fish and shellfish they expect to bring back, so that you can be there to buy it. Shellfish abound among the vast area of rocks visible at low tide off the coast (Roches de Grandcamp), especially scallops, oysters, mussels. Several fish restaurants on the quay.

HOTEL
Duguesclin, 4 quai Crampon (31.22.64.22): simple but attractive and lively Logis on quayside; good value meals, cheap rooms. ROOMS A–D. MEALS A–E. Shut 20–26 October, 15 January–6 February.

RESTAURANT
La Marée, quai Cheron (31.22.60.55): simple-looking restaurant on quayside with superb fish and excellent bouillabaisse. Very popular with yachtsmen. MEALS B–F. Shut 2–31 January; Monday, Wednesday evening.

GRANDCHAMP CHÂTEAU
[CALVADOS]

Moated manor (16th to 17th century) just off D511 SW of
Lisieux.

GRANVILLE
[MANCHE]

At the south end of the Cotentin's Atlantic coast, Granville is a
survivor of the days of French fishing off the Newfoundland
banks which started in the 16th century. Fishing died last century but Granville became a fashionable family resort and has
survived into the jet age. Its streets are steep, the beach at the
bottom of granite cliffs is narrow. But children love it because of
its busy port and its drawbridge leading to ramparts. A fifteen
minute walk along a cliff path takes you to an enormous beach at
Donville.

Haute-Ville, on the craggy headland, is a charming old town
of narrow streets between 18th-century houses leading up to the
solid, grey granite Notre-Dame church. The English founded
this fortified town on a rocky promontory stretching into the sea
in 1493 because they could not take Mont-St-Michel. But the
French took it three years later before it was finished. Granville
has boat connections with Jersey, Guernsey and little boats take
you in an hour to the offshore Chausey Isles (see page 110).

TOURIST INFORMATION Tourist Office, 15 rue
Clémenceau (33.50.02.67)
FESTIVALS February – From Saturday before Mardi
Gras (Shrove Tuesday) until Mardi Gras is held one of
the biggest carnivals in north France. July (last Sunday)
is a Pardon of blessing the sea with open air Mass, torch
procession and celebrations

HOTELS
Les Bains, Restaurant La Potinière, 19 rue Clémenceau

(33.50.17.31): grand old hotel, totally modernised, sound-proofed. Facing sea. 58 rooms have sea views. Lovely shellfish and sole. ROOMS C–E. MEALS B–E. Restaurant shut Monday in winter.

Normandy-Chaumière, 20 rue Paul-Poirier (33.50.01.71): in shopping area but owner is a good chef, excellent fish, splendid value. ROOMS C–D. MEALS A–E. Shut Christmas holidays; Tuesday evening, Wednesday except July, August.

Mougine des Moulins à Vent, at Bréville-sur-Mer, 4km NE (33.50.22.41): great house in flower gardens; no restaurant. ROOMS E–F. Open all year.

RESTAURANT

Phare, 11 rue Port (33.50.12.94): panoramic sea views; good fish. MEALS A–G. Shut 15–30 September, 20 December–30 January; Wednesday evening, Thursday.

HAMBYE ABBEY
[MANCHE]

The countryside of the Sienne valley and the hills around it to the north of Villedieu-les-Poêles is still serene and beautiful. It is easy to feel jealous of the Benedictine monks who lived here for centuries after Hambye Abbey was founded in 1145. Though the abbey started to decline in the 17th century and was broken up in the Revolution, there is still enough left of the vast church and the monastic buildings to imagine what it was like in its majestic days. Besides the shell of the Romanesque Gothic church, the surviving monastery buildings include a Gothic chapter house, a library, kitchen with a monumental fireplace and 14th-century wooden Christ, stable and a pigsty. The former refectory's walls are hung with tapestries and furnished with period pieces and the dormitory upstairs is still used for concerts (closed Tuesdays out of season).

Follow D258 for 9km east and you reach Mount Robin, with a calvary at its summit (276 metres) and long views.

HOTELS

Auberge de l'Abbaye (33.61.42.19): modest but delightful little hotel with excellent value meals. ROOMS A–B. MEALS A–D. Shut 1–6 October; Monday.

Restaurant de l'Abbaye (with bedrooms) (33.61.42.21): terrace overlooking river; very good meals with many ingredients fresh from owner's farm. Superb value. ROOMS (simple) A. MEALS A–C. Shut Wednesday.

Les Chevaliers, rue d'Estouteville D13 (33.90.42.09): simple village inn but good cooking and value. ROOMS (simple) A. MEALS A–E. Shut February; Sunday evening, Monday from 15 September–15 June.

HARCOURT-CHÂTEAU
[SEINE-MARITIME]

7km SE of Brionne on D137. The Harcourt family have not owned this château since the Revolution. They *do* own Champ-de-Bataille nearby (*see* page 109) which they lost in the Revolution to the state but which was returned to them after the 1944 wartime destruction of their château at Thury-Harcourt. Château Harcourt (13th to 14th centuries) was ruined in the Revolution but has been restored and has been owned since 1828 by the French Academy of Architecture. Forestry pioneer Louis Delamare established the forestry park around it and several trees planted in the last century are enormous (open afternoons 1 March–15 November except Tuesday).

HARFLEUR
[*see* Le Havre, page 38]

HÉRICOURT-EN-CAUX
[SEINE-MARITIME]

Pleasant farming village in the Durdent valley NW of Yvetot in
countryside where hamlets and farms have many old Norman
black-and-white timbered buildings. Interesting 18th-century
chapel. The Durdent, which runs through the village, is rich in
trout and there are trout farms nearby. It runs past the auberge
and an arm has been diverted under the dining room so
through a glass panel you can see trout swimming past your
table.

HOTEL

Auberge de la Durdent (35.96.42.44): simple bedrooms reached by
a little bridge over the river, simple bar, pleasant dining room;
friendly atmosphere. ROOMS B. MEALS A–D. Shut 10–28 February, 10–30 October.

HONFLEUR
[CALVADOS]

This remarkable and photogenic little port which has played an
important part in history, still bustles and hurries in the jet-
computer age. Absolutely delightful but crowded in summer.

An important port six hundred years ago, it rivalled Dieppe
in the 16th and 17th centuries for producing explorers and
corsairs. One, de Gonneville, is said to have reached Australia in
1503. A century later Samuel de Champlain sailed from Honfleur to colonise Canada and founded Québec in 1608. The first
four thousand colonists were nearly all Normans and Percherons. In 1665, one thousand soldiers were sent to protect the
colonists against the Iroquois Indians, who objected to their land
and hunting forests being stolen. A decree was then published
that they must marry within a fortnight one of the 'king's
daughters' sent out at the same time – peasant girls picked
mostly for sturdiness.

Honfleur fishing port

The inner harbour (Vieux Bassin) built in 1668 by Louis XIV for supplying France's American colonies, was replaced as the commercial dock a hundred years ago by another and is now a delightful scene. Used by yachtsmen and fishermen it is surrounded by tall, thin buildings, mostly with bars, restaurants, art galleries or antique shops at ground level. Though others, including the English painters Turner and Bonnington, were struck by the effect of light and sea and had painted this coast, it was the son of an Honfleur pilot born here in 1824, Eugène Boudin, who really began the fashion for painting seas and skyscapes. His meetings with other painters to drink cider in a farmhouse inn led to the birth of Impressionism. He was the centre of a group who met at Ferme St Siméon. Monet (whom Boudin had encouraged), Sisley, Pissarro, Cézanne and Corot gathered there. Courbet painted *The Garden of Mère Toutain*, who owned the inn. Dufy was inspired by Honfleur. But Boudin himself was not really appreciated until he was old. The Hon-

fleur museum in place Erik Satie is named after him and some of
his paintings are shown but there are better ones by Dufy,
Monet, Courbet and Jonkind. The museum has also some good
old Norman furniture, costumes and head-dresses (open
Easter–September daily, then Saturday and Sunday mornings
October–Easter).

These days, poor Boudin could certainly not have afforded
to eat or drink at Ferme St Siméon, which is one of the dearest
hotels and restaurants in Normandy. But it is a lovely example
of 17th-century rustic Norman building and its *manoir* 300
metres away is grandly Norman.

The market is held in place Ste Catherine around the
wooden church. It's fun to think that this church was built at
great speed by local craftsmen to thank God for getting rid of
the English! It was 1468, the end of the Hundred Years War,
Honfleur was ruined and impoverished after English occupation, stonemasons were busy rebuilding all over France. So local
shipwrights built a 'temporary' church of timber from Touques
forest. It is still there – with carved panels in the organ gallery
showing a group of angels playing seventeen different instruments. When Parisians flock to Honfleur on summer weekends,
you can retire to the beauty of Côte de Grâce Hill, with panoramic views over the Seine estuary, a mariners' chapel and
restaurants.

TOURIST INFORMATION Tourist Office, 33 cours Fossés
(31.89.23.30)
MARKET Saturday

HOTELS

Honfleur hotels are rather overpriced and many demand *demi-
pension* in summer.

Ferme St Siméon et son Manoir, route A.Marais (31.89.23.61): *see
above*. ROOMS G-plus. MEALS G-plus.

Cheval Blanc, 2 quai des Passagers (hotel 31.89.13.49 – restaurant 31.89.39.87): old favourite not quite so good now hotel and
restaurant are split. 15th-century posthouse; luxurious décor.
ROOMS E–G (hotel shut January). MEALS D–G (restaurant shut
4 January–6 March; Thursday).

Hostellerie Lechat, 3 place Catherine (31.89.23.85): in square by
the wooden church; 16th-century façade; they like you to dine
in. ROOMS C–F. MEALS C–G. Shut 4 January–5 February. Restaurant shut Wednesday, Thursday lunch.
Belvédère, 36 rue Emile Renouf (31.89.08.13): big old house in
gardens; flowery terrace. Quiet rooms. ROOMS B–C. MEALS
B–F. Shut 12–18 December, 4–15 January; Monday low season.
Auberge de la Source, at Barneville-le-Bertran, 6km SW
(31.89.25.02): best place to stay for Honfleur (6km) and
Deauville (10km); just inland; charming country hotel with
pleasant garden and trout pond in a nice village in lovely
countryside. Excellent fish. All bedrooms with private plumbing.
Half-board preferred. ROOMS C–E. MEALS C plus carte. Shut
mid-November–mid-February; Wednesday (except hotel in
July-August).

HOULGATE
[CALVADOS]

A very pleasant little resort above Dives-sur-Mer for old-style
family holidays. The superb long sands are backed by a promenade which continues to the bottom of the jagged Vaches
Noires cliffs, a haunt of fishermen, shrimpers, hunters of
shellfish and junior geologists seeking fossils. There are good
coastal views from the clifftops. The town itself has shady
avenues, still lined mainly with older houses and gardens, and
the countryside around it is most attractive.
TOURIST INFORMATION boul. des Belges (31.91.33.09)
– shut Saturday, Sunday.

HOTELS
La Ferme des Aulnettes, route de la Corniche (31.91.22.28): very
nice Norman-style restaurant; simple rooms. ROOMS B. MEALS
C–F. Shut 1–25 October, 25 November–25 March; Tuesday low
season.
Hotel 1900, 17 rue Bains (31.91.07.77): Logis with Casserole for

good, regional cooking. ROOMS B–E. MEALS A–F. Shut 4 January–6 February; Monday evening, Tuesday low season.

ISIGNY-SUR-MER
[CALVADOS]

Tucked away in an estuary of the Aure river in the Baie-des-Veys where Calvados meets the Cotentin peninsula, Isigny has a little quay where fishing boats land shellfish in baskets. But it is really a pleasant country market town, centre of the dairy industry since the 17th century. The best restaurants in France boast that they serve Isigny butter and cream. It is *présalé* land, too, among sea-washed salt meadows which produce the best lambs. A good place to eat or to shop for food. Restaurants are simple, but serve good meals. It was much damaged before the Americans liberated it on 9 June 1944, but the 13th-century tower and choir of the church survived. So did the 18th-century château which is now the town hall.

TOURIST INFORMATION Mairie (31.21.46.00)

MARKET Every 2nd Saturday

HOTELS

France, 15 rue E. Demagny (31.22.00.33): creeper-covered Logis built round a courtyard which hushes traffic noise but is used for parking. Practical air-conditioned bedrooms; excellent meals; good value. ROOMS B–D. MEALS A–C. Shut 15 November–15 February; Thursday evening, Saturday lunch except high summer.

Commerce, 5 rue E. Demagny (31.22.01.44): simple auberge with very good regional cooking. ROOMS A–C. MEALS A–C. Shut February; Sunday evening, Monday lunch low-season.

IVRY-LA-BATAILLE
[EURE]

On the river Eure. The battle was in 1590 when Henri IV defeated the Catholic League forces under the Duc de Mayenne. In 1804 Napoleon put up an obelisk to celebrate this victory. It is 7km NW (reached by D833, D163). The restored 16th-century church is attributed to Philibert Delorme, architect of the Tuileries in Paris. There are some fine half-timbered houses. Cross the river 3½km south into Eure-et-Loir and you find Château D'Anet, a truly beautiful building put up in 1548, under the direction of Delorme, by Henri II of France for his mistress Diane de Poitiers. The tympanum of the magnificent monumental doorway carries a cast of the Nymphe of Fontainebleau. The original, now in the Louvre, was by the great sculptor and self-publicist Benvenuto Cellini.

MARKETS Wednesday, Saturday

RESTAURANT
Moulin d'Ivry, 10 rue Henri IV (32.36.40.51): delightful; on river banks; classic Normandy dishes. Changed hands in 1988. MEALS D–F. Shut February; Sunday evening, Monday.

JULLOUVILLE
[MANCHE]

6km south of Granville, a rather superior little resort with fine sands, dunes and pleasant houses among pine trees. Visitors almost exclusively French.

TOURIST INFORMATION Syndicat d'Initiative
(33.61.82.48 – July, August)

HOTELS
Casino (33.61.82.82): period-piece seaside hotel of great charm. ROOMS C–D. MEALS C–D. Shut January, February; Tuesday mid-September to 1 June.

JUMIÈGES ABBEY
[SEINE-MARITIME]

Glorious ruins beside the Seine 16km upriver from Caudebec. Towers are truncated, bays are gaping open, vaults have collapsed, but still the beauty of Romanesque architecture shines forth in dignity, especially in sunshine. Massive pillars and arches still tower to 27 metres high. Most of the remains are of the building of 1040. The builder, the Benedictine Abbot Robert Champart, was made Archbishop of Canterbury by Edward the Confessor and then showered English riches into his Norman abbey. He died in 1052 and was buried beneath the chancel. The finished abbey was consecrated in 1067 with great pomp before William the Conqueror, who presented the monks

Ruins, Jumieges Abbey

with Hayling Island ('Holy Island') in Hampshire. The original abbey had been founded 400 years earlier by St Philibert, but that one was repeatedly pillaged and burned by Norsemen sailing up the Seine. The abbey was closed in 1791 under the Revolutionary Council and auctioned. A timber merchant bought it and used it as a stone-quarry. What was left was saved by a new owner in 1852 and now belongs to the nation (closed Tuesdays).

To appreciate Jumièges, take the nearby car-ferry (*bac*) and see it from across the river from D143.

LESSAY
[MANCHE]

A little town at the mouth of the river Ay halfway up the west coast of the Manche, Lessay has a nearly perfect Romanesque abbey-church – a masterpiece in glowing, golden stone. It was founded in 1050, escaped destruction even in the Revolution but not in 1944, when it was wrecked. In its restoration, every piece of original material which could be salvaged was used. Craftsmen even worked with tools like those used in mediaeval times. In 1864, the writer, Barbey d'Aurevilly, deplored the abbey's plain glass. Now it has windows in grey, ochre and yellow inspired by Irish Celtic manuscripts. There is a new pebble mosaic floor in the baptistry and a high altar which is a monolithic slab on two massive supports.

Every September since the 13th century, St Cross Fair has been held in Lessay – the biggest and most traditional fair in Normandy. Tents are erected around the countryside for vast horse and sheepdog sales. It lasts for four days around the second weekend in September. Sheep and geese are roasted in the open air and music and dancing continue into the night.

LILLEBONNE
[SEINE-MARITIME]

Just a little industrial town now, 10km NE of the Tancarville Bridge, but had moments of glory under Julius Caesar, as the military town of Juliobonna, and was capital of the area's Gauloise tribes, with a population of 25,000 (now it is 10,000). It was a main Roman port until it silted up later. The layout of a 2nd-century Roman theatre which held 10,000 people can be clearly followed, even to the vomitorium, and there is a Gallic-Roman museum in the town hall (open afternoons May–31 August; otherwise Sunday afternoons). In the castle William the Bastard, Duke of Normandy, assembled the barons and persuaded them to invade England. The castle was rebuilt in the 12th century. There remains one wall and a round tower which you can climb (109 steps).

LION-SUR-MER
[CALVADOS]

Family resort 5km W of Ouistreham with extensive rocks (Les Roches de Lion) uncovered at low tide. Church is partly 12th and 13th century. A 16th-century château with Renaissance pavilion in a park is not open to the public.

LISIEUX
[CALVADOS]

Though now the most important and thriving industrial town in the rich Auge, Lisieux is still known for the gentle Ste Thérèse. Thérèse Martin was born in Alençon in 1873 but when her mother died her father moved to Lisieux. She decided when she was nine to become a nun. At fourteen she was refused entry to the local Carmelite convent, so she made a pilgrimage to Rome and asked the Pope, who gave her special permission.

In 1897, just before she entered hospital to die painfully of TB, this 24-year-old girl completed her life story, called the *Story of a Soul*. She promised to spend her time in heaven letting a 'rain of roses' fall on the earth. Her book was a great success, especially a later, edited version. She was canonised in 1925 and the cult has grown fast. Her home *Les Buissonets* is a museum, with the games of her childhood and communion robe on view. Her remains are enshrined in a glass casket containing her effigy in the simple chapel of the Carmelite convent and in 1954 they completed a massive lofty new Byzantine basilica to the south of Lisieux, built to accommodate tens of thousands of pilgrims who came all the year from all over the world. Mosaics and coloured windows tell the story of her life, but it is hardly a beautiful or elegant building. In season a little train runs between her home and the basilica and there is a Son-et-Lumière of her life (early June–end September 9.30 p.m.).

Long ago Lisieux was called a cathedral city but the church of St Pierre, completed in the 13th century and said to be the first Norman-Gothic church of France, lost its cathedral status at the end of the 18th century. It is an architectural jewel. The Flamboyant Lady Chapel was rebuilt in the 15th century on orders of Pierre Cauchon, who became Bishop of Lisieux after being one of the judges who condemned Joan of Arc to death. The lantern tower is 15th-century, too. The church of St Désir has a bold colourful window by Max Ingrand.

6km S at St Germain-de-Livet is a delicious château surrounded by a moat. Built in the 15th and 16th centuries in Italian Renaissance style, it has a delightful chequered pattern in sandstone and green-varnished brick, and has been called 'a castle of ivory starred with emeralds'. It has a great tower with pepper-pot roof, two thinner towers flanking the doorway, and at one end, like an extension, a typical timber-framed Norman manor. It is built round a courtyard with an arcaded gallery and is just as delightful inside. The guard room contains 16th-century frescos of battle scenes. The dining room has a beautiful fireplace and Empire-period furniture. A gallery in the 16th-century wing has paintings by the Riesener family, better known as cabinet-makers and decorators in marquetry in Louis XVI's court. Well worth visiting (castle shut Tuesday).

St Germain-de-Livet

The renowned Père Jules Calvados distillery on Route de Dives, sells calvados and Vallée d'Auge cider (31.79.20.53).

TOURIST INFORMATION 11 rue d'Alençon (31.62.08.41)

FESTIVALS Sunday nearest 15 July – consecration of Basilica of Ste Thérèse. Mid-August – procession of the Smiling Virgin. September (last Sunday) – Festival of Ste Thérèse (her shrine is carried in procession)

HOTEL

La Coupe d'Or, 49 rue Pont-Mortain (31.31.16.84): Logis de France; comfortable. Nice regional cooking at sensible prices.

Rooms C–E. Meals A–F. Restaurant only shut 15 December–
15 January.

Parc, 21 boul. Herbert-Fournet (31.62.08.11): in the music room
of a château. Modern cooking but not excessively so. Meals
B–F. Shut 25 January to mid-February; Tuesday evening, Wednesday.
Ferme du Roy, 122 boul. Herbert-Fournet (31.31.33.98): décor of
an old Norman farm. Good traditional regional dishes. Good
value. Meals B–F. Shut mid-December to mid-January; Sunday
evening, Monday.

LISORES
[Calvados]

Hamlet 3km N of Vimoutiers. Just outside is a barn converted
into a museum of the life and work of the artist Fernand Léger
(1881–1955). Among exhibits are bronzes and rugs and tapestries in his distinctive style which he called 'aesthetic of the
machine'. He used to stay on the farm on his holidays.

LIVAROT
[Calvados]

Little town 18km SW of Lisieux in the Vie valley where the
superb pungent cheese is made (*see* Cheeses page 11), also excellent butter. Some fine old houses. At the Conservatoire des
Techniques Fromagères (16 rue l'Évêque) they use the old
methods to make camembert, Pont l'Évêque and Livarot, wrap-
ping the Livarot in reeds from the bank of the river Vie. Most
makers now wrap it in waxed paper. For a small fee you can tour
the dairy and taste the cheeses. You can also eat from a range of
fixed-price menus in the café and buy cheese. There is a calvados and cider maker in town.

LONGNY-AU-PERCHE
[ORNE]

A good centre for touring the Normandy Perche, a land of meadows, manor houses, lakes, large forests of oaks and beech, and once home of Percheron horses until they were replaced by farm machines. Longny is a rival to Caen as the home of tripe. A national contest for the best dish of tripe is held on 1 May. Delightful Renaissance chapel of Notre-Dame-de-Pitié in the cemetery. A statue of Our Lady of Mercy on the high altar is claimed to have performed miracles. There is a pilgrimage on 8 September. Horse fairs are still held but are not so important now.

TOURIST INFORMATION Hotel de Ville (33.73.65.42)
MARKET Wednesday

HOTEL
France, 6 rue de Paris (33.73.64.11): Logis de France. ROOMS B–C. MEALS A–F. Shut 15–30 January; Sunday evening, Monday.

LOUVIERS
[EURE]

Light industry and the A13 motorway passing nearby the northern edge of Louviers have done much to destroy its tranquillity. But the old quarter still has some beautiful old houses and you can still fish from green banks in the several arms of the Eure river which run through the town. Timbered houses are in rues Tatin, Pierre-Mendez-France and du Quai. The TOURIST OFFICE is in Maison du Fou du Roy, the house of a master apothecary who became court-jester to Henri IV after his famous fool Chicot was killed in battle. The broken arches of the cloisters of an Italianate 17th-century Convent of the Penitents are the only cloisters in Europe built over water. But the famous building is the great church of Notre Dame, built in the 13th century but given a Flamboyant south face in the 15th century. The masons who shaped the stone into the delicate swirls, festoons, openwork and pinnacles must have been great artists in their own right. The inside contains interesting works of art, including two Nottingham alabaster panels, stained glass from the 15th and 16th centuries and a good *Adoration of the Magi* by a local artist Jean Nicole. The museum includes some excellent Rouen porcelain (closed Tuesday).

A fascinating new museum in the town hall is devoted to theatre and opera scenery and film sets of Georges Wakhevitch (1907–84) who lived at Tosny between Louviers and Les Andelys. He designed sets for some of the greatest films and theatre productions, including sets for Jean Cocteau, Peter Brook, Jean Renoir and Sir Laurence Olivier, and for operas all over the world. There are more than 150 models in tableau form of his sets, showing scenery, actors and costumes, and many drawings for scenery and costume. The plan is to make a museum of the work of all the great designers of stage and screen.

Louviers made woollen garments from the 13th century until the 1970s.

TOURIST INFORMATION 10 rue Maréchal-Foch
(32.40.04.41)
MARKET Wednesday, Saturday
FESTIVALS September – Fair of St Michel

HOTELS

Auberge de la Haye le Comte, 4 route de la Haye le Comte, off D113 S of Louviers (32.40.00.40): fine old Norman house in gardens; bed and breakfast only. ROOMS C–D. Shut 1 November–30 April.

Les Saisons, at Vironvay, 5km SE by N155, left on N15 (32.40.02.56): bungalows in gardens in a small village; good cooking – pricey. ROOMS F. MEALS C–G. Shut 8–26 February; 16–26 August. Restaurant shut Monday.

LUC-SUR-MER
[CALVADOS]

Seaside resort 10km W of Ouistreham with 2km promenade above a sandy beach. Rocks at low tide covered in seaweed. A spa offering hydrosodium iodate treatment, Thalasso Thérapie, rue Guynemer (31.97.32.22). Low cliffs have caves which you can reach at low tide. Attractive park.

TOURIST INFORMATION Syndicat d'Initiative, place Petit-Enfer (15 June–15 September – 31.97.33.25).

HOTELS
Beau Rivage, 1 rue Charcot (31.96.49.51): probably the best hotel here. ROOMS B–E. MEALS A–F. Shut 1 October–22 March.
Marsouin, 2 rue Charcot (31.97.32.08): Logis with casserole for good regional cooking. ROOMS B–D. MEALS A–G. Shut mid-November–mid-February; Sunday evening, Monday low season.

LYONS-LA-FORÊT
[EURE]

An old hunting forest of the Dukes of Normandy. Once jealously preserved, it still has 100 square kilometres of magnificent beeches and oaks, and is a delight for driving the small roads or walking forest tracks. Trees grow to enormous heights in the chalky soil. In the middle is the old foresters' village of Lyons-la-Forêt grown into a little town of eight hundred people, still very pretty and tranquil despite inevitable summer visitors. Old timbered buildings, many of them once woodsmen's houses, are prettily restored and colour washed, and in the middle is a market hall with a sturdy 18th-century oak roof cut from ancient oaks of the forest. The 15th-century church has a wooden belfry and large wooden statues.

It was at Lyons that Henry I of England died after the historic 'surfeit of lampreys', eaten the previous night at the

Abbey of Mortemer 4km S. Probably he ate these little eels with the poisonous black thread still in them. The ruins of the Cistercian abbey are in a woodland setting, part of a farm. The Conventual building, reconstructed in the 17th century, has a museum of monastic life (open afternoons from Easter–mid-September, Sunday afternoon the rest of the year). A little train takes you on a tour, including the little lake where the lampreys probably came from. Lyons forest was used by French guerillas fighting the English in the Hundred Years War, and as a dropping zone by the RAF for the Resistance in World War Two.

TOURIST INFORMATION Mairie (32.49.60.87 – shut Sunday, Monday)

MARKET Thursday

FESTIVAL Thursday after 9 October – St Octave de la Fête Dieu

HOTELS

La Licorne (32.49.62.02): delightful, very popular traditional old inn; excellent classic cooking. ROOMS E–F. MEALS C–F. Shut 15 December–21 January; Sunday evening, and Monday in winter.

Domaine St Paul, on N321 route Tronquay (32.49.60.57): peaceful country Logis. ROOMS C–E. MEALS C. Shut mid-November to mid-March.

Grand Cerf (32.49.60.44): very attractive auberge. Good, Norman fish dishes. Expensive meals. ROOMS C–E. MEALS F. Shut mid-January–mid-February; Tuesday, Wednesday.

MANÉGLISE
[SEINE-MARITIME]

Village in Lézarde valley 3½km from Epouville, inland between Étretat and Le Havre. Lovely tiny Romanesque church – one of the best in France – with a minute 12th-century nave.

MARTAINVILLE
[SEINE-MARITIME]

12km E of Rouen on N31, a village near Lyons forest with a château built between 1485 and 1510 by a rich merchant. In stone and brick with a massive 16th-century pigeon loft and 18th-century half-timbered barn, it is unusually attractive. The big brick chimneys have Gothic decoration outside and beautiful fireplaces within. It is now a museum of Norman traditions and arts, and contains fine old furniture (15th to 19th centuries) and costumes (shut Tuesday, Wednesday).

MESNIÈRES-EN-BRAY
[SEINE-MARITIME]

Between D1 and the Béthune river, NW of Neufchâtel-en-Bray, it has a majestically beautiful Renaissance château which looks defendable. But its massive towers are ornamental to give it prestige, for it was built in the 14th century as a house. An 18th-century grand staircase leads to the main courtyard. Many rooms are ornamented and the gallery is decorated with carved stags. Chapel in one tower still has 16th-century glass. It is a college now, but open Sunday and Saturday afternoon Easter–end of September.

MESNIL VAL
[see Criel Plage, page 119]

MOLAY-LITTRY
[CALVADOS]

Quiet village beside Cerisy forest 14km SW Bayeaux by D5. Mining museum traces evolution of coal mining here. (Open 1

April–30 September except Wednesday; rest of year all day Sunday, afternoons Tuesday, Saturday.) Mines closed in 1950.

HOTEL

Château du Molay, route d'Isigny D5 (31.22.90.82): handsome, massive 18th-century château in lovely grounds with pool, small river, deer. Luxurious. Excellent cooking. ROOMS E–G. MEALS D–G. Shut 1 December–1 March.

MONDAYE ABBEY
[CALVADOS]

10km S of Bayeux: ancient monastery rebuilt in the 18th century by the prior Eustache Restout who was both architect and decorator of the abbey and church. He was the uncle of the painter Jean Restout. Decorations are unusual, especially the large terracotta group in the Lady Chapel (open 14 July–31 August weekdays; rest of year Sunday).

MONT DES AVALOIRS
[ORNE]

15km W of Alençon in the centre of Multonne forest. A metal belvedere at the top is 417 metres high, the highest point in Western France. Wide views over Monaye and Écouve forests, Alençon countryside, and the Perche hills, with the Mancelle Alps on the horizon.

MONTPINCHON
[MANCHE]

13km SE Coutances. The Bishops of Coutances lived in the Château de la Salle and kept an eye on their cathedral by having all the land cleared in between! Now an hotel – a hideout from the crowds of Mont-St-Michel (*see below*).

HOTEL
Château de la Salle (33.46.95.19): beautiful, elegantly furnished, expensive and worth the money. 13th-century vaulted dining-room, open fires. ROOMS G. MEALS D–F. Open 20 March–early November; Friday, Saturday only in November, December.

MONT-ST-MICHEL
[*see Sites*, page 53]

MORTAGNE-AU-PERCHE
[ORNE]

Its citizens used to boast 'Mortagne on the mountains, the most beautiful town in France'. It is high on a mound, with panoramic views of a green and wooded landscape of valleys. Its brown-tiled houses are clustered around the hill and from its public gardens behind the town hall, in which stands a huge bronze of a Percheron horse, are magnificent views to the Perseigne forest. It is a pleasant little town and the approach through the Perche forest from the north on D930 passing little lakes is delightful. Notre Dame church (1493–1535) is a combination of Flamboyant Gothic and early Renaissance styles 'with a resultant loss of unity in the exterior' says Michelin politely. It looks lop-sided and the heavy 19th-century tower doesn't help. But inside are superb wood carvings brought from the Valdieu Carthusian monastery in nearby Reno forest when it was closed. Mortagne, like Bellême, is a good centre for touring the Normandy Perche.

Mortagne is famous for its smoked *boudin-noir* (blood sausage) and an international black pudding contest is held on the first Sunday after mid-Lent. Competitors come from all over Western Europe, including Britain, and Lancashire pudding makers have won prizes, beating even the Germans. It's a serious affair, with enormous consumption over three days, and there are eating contests. Buy *boudin* at Charcuterie Maurice Batrel, 52 place Général-de-Gaulle.

TOURIST INFORMATION place Général-de-Gaulle
(33.25.04.22) – in season
MARKET Saturday morning
FESTIVALS June – music

HOTELS

Tribunal, 4 place du Palais (33.25.04.77): in a charming old house of 13th and 18th centuries; good value meals with classical cooking using local ingredients. ROOMS B–E. MEALS A–E. Open all year.

Hostellerie Genty-Home, 4 rue Notre Dame (33.25.11.53): another good restaurant in an old stone house, with good, classical regional cooking. ROOMS C–E. MEALS A–F. Shut Monday.

MORTAIN
[MANCHE]

Halfway up a rocky hillside in beautiful surroundings among deep forest land and lovely waterfalls of the river Cance, Mortain had to be rebuilt after a German counter-attack in August 1944. Waters of the Grande Cascade among woodlands fall 25 metres. The Petite Cascade waters fall 35 metres but are not so spectacular. Near Grande Cascade is the 12th to 13th-century Cistercian Abbaye Blanche, with a large beautifully proportioned Romanesque cloister. It isn't white – the monks wore white habits. The town is rather dominated by the 13th-century Gothic limestone St Evroult church, but it is severe and not very interesting except for its Romanesque doorway. The joy of Mortain is following marked woodland paths crossing streams on little wooden bridges and stepping stones.

TOURIST INFORMATION 1 rue Bourg-Lopin (in season
– 33.59.00.51)
MARKET Saturday

HOTELS

Poste, 1 place des Arcades (33.59.00.05): pleasant; good value. ROOMS B–C. MEALS A–C. Shut 20 December–1 February; Friday evening, Saturday.

Cascades, 16 rue Bassin (33.59.00.03): excellent value meals. ROOMS A–C. MEALS A–D. Shut 20 December–3 January; Sunday evening, Monday.

NACQUEVILLE CHÂTEAU
[MANCHE]

9km W of Cherbourg on D45, turn left at hamlet of La Rivière. Attractively situated and beautiful 16th-century manor house is set in a park with fine beech trees and superb flowers, some semi-tropical. At its best in May and June. You can visit only the great hall of the house, with a beautiful Renaissance fireplace (afternoons Easter–30 September except Tuesday, Friday).

NEUFCHÂTEL-EN-BRAY
[SEINE-MARITIME]

Centre of the Bray area, still called 'the dairy of Paris', even if you no longer 'smell cheese in every room of your inn', as the English poet and critic Francis Palgrave wrote last century. The main cheese is *bondon*, soft, white, packed in straw in all sorts of shapes from cylinders to hearts, delicate when young, strong when mature. It is still made mostly on farms and distributed in Neufchâtel. They also make *Petit Suisse* cheese. Neufchâtel was bombed heavily by the Germans in 1940 and the restoration of the vast Notre Dame church in its centre is only just completed. Mostly Gothic (13th to 16th centuries). The Mathon-Durand museum in a 16th-century house has interesting exhibits of local arts and crafts including a cider mill of 1746, and cider press from 1837. (Open afternoons in season, Saturday and Sunday afternoons low season).

MARKET Tuesday and Saturday morning

HOTEL

Les Airelles, 2 passage Michu (35.93.14.60): ROOMS A–D. MEALS A–C. Shut 15–31 October, part February; Wednesday.

O, CHÂTEAU D'
[ORNE]

Château d'O

Near Montrée, 8km NW of Sées. A truly delightful, almost fairy-tale castle seeming to rise magically from the waters of its lake with a wide moat around so that it appears to be built on an island. You pass under a portal into a courtyard with three pavilions. The oldest is Gothic from the end of the 15th century. Its walls are chequered in brick and stone, its graceful turrets and sloping roofs are charming. The early Renaissance south wing, added a year later, is of one storey with big windows opening onto the countryside. The delicate columns of its arcade show the emblems of Jean d'O, whose family gave the castle its name. The façade of the West wing is of Henri IV's time but the inside, the main living quarters, were entirely rebuilt in the 18th century. You can see the kitchen, the hallway, a grand staircase and several rooms with interesting furnishings, including a superb Grand Salon. The large park is delightful – superb for picnics. Or you can eat in a good restaurant in the old stables. There are swans on the moat, doves in the lofts and fish rising in the lake. A lovely spot. Château d'O is one of the nicest places to visit in Normandy (Château open afternoons except February and Tuesdays).

RESTAURANT

La Ferme d'O, (33.35.35.27): very pleasant. Traditional cooking with regional ingredients. MEALS A–E. Shut 10 January–28 February; Tuesday lunch in mid-summer; Sunday evening, Tuesday rest of year.

OFFRANVILLE
[SEINE-MARITIME]

Village with avenue of beeches 8km SW of Dieppe. In the church, built in 1517, is a memorial tableau of a soldier being buried in the 1914–18 War. It is by the painter Jacques-Emile Blanche (1861–1941) who lived and died in the local Manoir du Tôt. He was married to an English woman and his studio became the centre of an Anglo-French colony of artists and writers from the 1880s until the late 1930s. He painted mostly portraits of leading writers, musicians, intellectuals (his tableau includes the leading personalities of Offranville) and he was a respected writer on art, too. A large collection of his portraits (including those of André Gide, Cocteau and Stravinsky) is in Rouen's Musée des Beaux Arts (*see* page 33).

ORBEC
[CALVADOS]

A lively, interesting town in a beautiful wooded valley in the Auge, and a good centre for exploring the delightful Auge countryside and hamlets hidden on little roads. Orbec is 20km SE of Lisieux and few foreigners seem to know that it exists. Nor do they know of the river Orbiquet which springs from the ground 5km away near La Folletière-Abenon. Along Grande Rue are old houses with wooden gables, courtyards and flowers. They inspired Debussy to write *Jardins sous la Pluie* ('Gardens in the Rain').

Notre Dame church has a massive tower built in the 15th and 16th centuries. The 16th-century glass was well restored after World War Two.

You can buy camembert cheese, calvados and cider direct from farms around here. Camembert is made, too, at Lanquetot, a shop-factory at 8 rue de Vimoutiers.

TOURIST INFORMATION Mairie (31.32.73.38)
MARKET Wednesday

HOTEL
France, 152 rue Grande (31.32.74.02): 18th-century coaching post-house, well-run; rooms in annexe better and dearer than in old relais. Good fresh local products. ROOMS A–E. MEALS B–D. Shut mid-December–mid-January.

RESTAURANT
Au Caneton, 32 rue Grande (31.32.73.32): famed for enormous Norman meals, with good portions; ingredients from local farms; superb duck dishes and cheese board. Not cheap but

excellent. In attractive surroundings of a 17th-century house with beams and brass. MEALS F–G. Shut February, October; Monday evening, Tuesday.

ORIVAL
[SEINE-MARITIME]

South of Rouen but upriver on the Seine are Rochers d'Orival (Orival Rocks). The path to them from the road is steep and slippery when wet. It passes caves hollowed out of the rock and leads to fine views of the Seine. Orival village 1½km S has an odd half-troglodyte 15th-century church. The Seine here is very attractive.

OUISTREHAM
[CALVADOS]

The port for Caen destroyed in 1944 has truly risen from the ashes, especially since Brittany Ferries started their car ferry service from Portsmouth. It is linked to Caen by a canal dug last century parallel to the Orne river, now used extensively by yachts. Ouistreham is a yachting centre. Its very popular beach Riva Bella has superb sands. Here at dawn on 6 June 1944, the 4th Anglo-French Commando landed. A Landing Museum is open every day from June–September. Saturday and Sunday only from Palm Sunday–end of May. Long views of the coast from the lighthouse (30m high – visits afternoons 1 April–mid-September).

TOURIST INFORMATION Tourist Office, Jardins du
Casino (1 June–15 October – 31.97.18.63)

HOTELS
Univers, Broche d'Argent Restaurant, place de Gaulle (31.97.12.16): very useful, pleasant hotel near ferry; big terrace

café, well-equipped little bedrooms (also annexe). Good shellfish. ROOMS C–D. MEALS A–F. Shut 23 December–3 January.

Normandie, 71 ave Michel–Cabieu (31.97.19.57): popular restaurant, excellent Norman cooking, especially of shellfish; bedrooms improved. ROOMS D–E. MEALS C–G. Shut 2–27 January; Sunday evening; Monday in winter.

PACY-SUR-EURE
[EURE]

18km E of Evreux; a good touring centre for Eure valley. St Aubin church altered in the 16th century, is Gothic with a superb nave and modern amber-coloured windows by Décorchemont. Also beautiful 16th-century stone statues.

TOURIST INFORMATION Mairie (32.36.03.27)

MARKET Thursday

HOTELS

Etape, 1 rue Isambard (32.36.12.77): big house on banks of Eure, garden to the river. ROOMS B–C. MEALS B–F. Shut January; Sunday evening, Monday.

La Ferme de Cocherel, at Cocherel, 6km NW (32.36.68.27): lovely old farmhouse beside the Eure with just three delightful bedrooms. Classical cooking. Lures Parisians, so pricey. ROOMS F. MEALS D (weekdays), G. Shut Tuesday, Wednesday.

Château de Brécourt, at Douains, 6km NE (32.52.40.50): one of the superb Savry family hotels; big Louis XIII château beautifully renovated. Relais et Châteaux hotel. Excellent cooking by new chef. Expensive. ROOMS F–G. MEALS F–G. Open all year.

PIN-AU-HARAS (Haras du Pin)
[ORNE]

12km E of Argentan. One of the most important studs in Europe, in a deliciously graceful château and stables, designed by Louis XIV's architect Mansart in 1716 in the heart of a lovely forest. It has been called the horses' Versailles. It was planned by the astute and crafty politician Colbert to improve the breed of French horses (probably for the cavalry – he was aiming for revenge on England after French defeats). Well over a hundred stallions, including many from Ireland and England. The Duke of Edinburgh has driven his carriage team in competition there. Its most famous horse Furioso came from England in 1946, died in 1967, having sired many racing and show jumping champions, including Olympic and World champions. His descendants are still prized at sales. (Conducted tours morning and afternoon).

PONT AUDEMER
[EURE]

Attractive former port on several little waterways, branches of river Risle. Many old half-timbered and stone riverside houses escaped war damage, so did old streets, little bridges and courtyards off rue République. Some houses have wrought iron balconies overhanging the water.

St Ouen's church, started in the 11th century, enlarged in the 16th century, has superb Renaissance glass and modern windows in reds and greens which are striking even by Max Ingrand's standards.

The old inn, Auberge du Vieux Puits, is one of the finest old buildings, inside and out. Good view of the river from Bras Sud bridge. Pont Audemer claims to have invented the sausage.

TOURIST INFORMATION Tourist Office, place Maubert
(32.41.08.21)

MARKET Excellent, down main street which is closed –
Monday and Friday

HOTELS

Auberge du Vieux Puits, 6 rue Notre Dame du Pré (32.41.01.48):
sheer delight. New rooms added carefully have not harmed the
17th-century house nor charming garden. Traditional dishes,
many Norman. Antiques, engravings, beams, flagstones, huge
fires. If staying you must take dinner. Meals pricey but excellent.
ROOMS B–F. MEALS F–G. Shut 27 June–7 July, 18 December–
19 January; Monday evening, Tuesday.

RESTAURANT

La Frégate, 4 rue Seüle (32.41.12.03): in beautiful old house in
noisy street. Very palatable meals. MEALS C–F. Shut mid July–1
August; Tuesday lunch, Wednesday.

Half-timbered houses, Pont Audemer

PONT DE L'ARCHE
[EURE]

Takes its name from first bridge built across the Lower Seine
(9th century) even before Rouen had a bridge. It is in a valley in
which the Seine meets the Eure, on the edge of Bord Forest with
a background of pines. The Flamboyant church of Notre-Dame-
des-Arts (1500–85) has stained glass from the 16th and 17th
centuries and fine furnishings including choir stalls brought
from the now-ruined Bonport Abbey 2km W. This was built by
Richard Coeur de Lion in 1190 to fulfil a vow made when he
escaped drowning when swimming in the Seine with his horse.

PONT D'OUILLY
[CALVADOS]

At the meeting of the Orne and Noireau rivers and at the centre
of Suisse-Normande. 3km south on D167 turn left on D43 to see
Méandre de Rouvrou, a spectacular bend in the river. A few
kilometres along D301 is Roche d'Oêtre, a rock 120 metres
above the winding wooden Rouvre gorges. Very spectacular.

HOTEL
Auberge St Christophe at St Christophe, 2km on D23
(31.69.81.23): quiet logis, pretty garden; path to Orne river.
Simple bedrooms, meals good value. ROOMS C. MEALS B–E.
Shut 25 September–21 October, February; Sunday evening,
Monday in winter.

PONT L'ÉVÊQUE
[CALVADOS]

Famous for its cheese since the 13th century. War damaged, so
few old houses remain. Hôtel de Ville and tourist information

centre are in an 18th-century mansion (Hôtel de Brilly) birthplace of the dramatist Robert de Flers (1872–1927).

TOURIST INFORMATION Mairie (31.64.12.77)

MARKET Monday

HOTEL

Lion d'Or, 8 place Calvaire (31.65.01.55): very good fish, well prepared. ROOMS C–D. MEALS C–E. Open every day.

Auberge de la Truite, at St-Martin-aux-Chartrains, 3.5km on N177 NW (31.65.21.64): little old country inn which excellent young chef Jean-Michel Lebon has made into a country retreat for gourmets staying at Deauville. Rustic rooms. ROOMS B–E. MEALS B–E. Shut February; Wednesday evening, Thursday except in August.

PONTÉCOULANT CHÂTEAU
[CALVADOS]

20km W of Pont d'Ouilly by D511, D105, D298. Surrounded by a landscaped park with two lakes, this charming little turreted château (16th to 18th centuries) has been turned into a museum by the Calvados *Département*, beautifully furnished like a family house (shut October, Tuesday and Monday in winter).

PONTORSON
[MANCHE]

Just inland on the Brittany border. Useful place to stay if visiting Mont-St-Michel. Many hotels. Notre Dame church founded by William the Conqueror in gratitude for saving his army from quicksands around the Mount (depicted on Bayeux tapestry and a window in this church). 15km E at St James is the cemetery of 4,410 Americans killed in 1944.

TOURIST INFORMATION Mairie (33.60.00.18)

HOTELS

Le Montgomery, 13 rue Couesnon (33.60.00.09): delightful France Accueil hotel in old home of the Counts of Montgomery. Beautiful old furniture and panelling. Pretty garden. Good regional cooking; *pré-salé* lamb. ROOMS C–D. MEALS A–G. Open 1 April–mid-October.

Bretagne, 59 rue Couesnon (33.60.10.55): charming, wood-framed 14th-century house, sympathetically furnished. ROOMS B–D. MEALS A–D. Shut 1 December–1 February except Christmas, New Year; Monday.

PONT-ST-PIERRE
[EURE]

Small attractive town spread along Andelle river valley, SW of Lyons forest, it has a photogenic 15th-century manor house (no visits) and an 11th to 12th-century church containing interesting furnishings and statues from Fontaine-Guérard Abbey, 3½km E. The abbey, though ruined, is attractive in its green and river setting. The lofty ruins of the abbey church, the chapter house and the monks' dormitory can still be seen (open afternoons except Mondays early April–end October). 4km SW is Côte des Deux Amants, a hill with magnificent views of the Seine Valley (*see* page 122). Écluses d'Amfreville (Amfreville Locks), just upstream from where the Andelle meets the Seine, control, with the Poses Dam, the flow of the Seine, dividing the canalised section from the free-flowing river which is affected by Channel tides. The big lock – 220 metres long by 17 metres will take 15 boats up to 38 metres long.

HOTEL

Bonne Marmite (32.49.70.24): comfortable rooms; attractive dining room with lobster tank. ROOMS E. MEALS D–E. Shut 25 July–mid-August, mid-February to mid-March; Saturday lunch, Friday, also Sunday evening in winter.

PORTBAIL
[Manche]

River, sea, sand dunes with little grey-stone harbour make this
attractive little place into a modest resort, though among tidal
flats. It lies south of Barneville-Carteret. 11th-century church
with 18th-century tower and ancient Gallo-Roman baptistry
(uncovered in 1956). From a tiny port across a causeway over the
Ollonde river estuary ferries leave for Jersey and Sark (Easter–
All Saints' Day).

HOTEL
La Galiche, place Edmond Laquaine (33.04.84.18): old regional
dishes (ham in cider and cream), shellfish. ROOMS (simple) A–C.
MEALS A–F. Shut 1–15 October, February; Sunday evening,
Monday except July, August.

PORT-EN-BESSIN
[Calvados]

On the edge of the Gold and Omaha Landing Beaches, 11km N
of Bayeux (*see* D-Day Beaches, page 57), and freed on 7 June by
47 Royal Marine Commando after a remarkable 20km march
through enemy territory; it is a lively, interesting fishing port
hidden between cliffs. A half-circle granite jetty forms an outer
fishing harbour where boats leave to catch scallops in the Seine
bay and white fish off Cornwall and Devon. The fish is sold on
the quayside in the early morning as it is landed. The jetty is a
haunt of line fishermen. A fort built by Vauban (17th-century)
stands guard on cliffs over the harbour end and you can climb
the rocks to a German *blockhaus* for a good view over the port.

HOTEL
La Marine, quai Letourneur (31.21.70.08): right on quayside;
excellent fish. ROOMS (simple) B–C. MEALS A–E. Shut 1
December–early February.

RESTAURANT

La Foncée, 12 rue Letourneur (31.21.71.66): pretty little restaurant; 'modern-regional cooking'. Good cheaper menu. MEALS C–F. Shut mid–end February; Tuesday, Wednesday.

PORT RACINE
[MANCHE]

Smallest port in France, cosily attractive; NW of Cherbourg on north coast of Cotentin Peninsula, usually placed under St Germain-des-Vaux in French books.

HOTEL

Hostellerie d'Erguillère, (33.52.75.31): Logis, quiet hideout. Flower garden with sea-view. Good cooking, quite pricey meals. ROOMS D–E. MEALS D–F. Shut January, February; Sunday evening, Monday except high season.

POURVILLE-SUR-MER
[SEINE-MARITIME]

Simple resort under cliffs 4km SW of Dieppe with large beach. Destroyed in the Anglo-Canadian Dieppe Raid of 1942. The Canadian Cameron Highlanders and South Saskatchewan Regiment landed here to the sound of their pipes, inflicted heavy German casualties and returned under Royal Navy protection though they lost their rearguard. At the beginning of the century it rivalled Dieppe as a fashionable resort and many artists and writers stayed there, including Maupassant, Renoir, Monet, Proust, Debussy (after he left Puys), and later Cocteau. Here Renoir painted *Madame Charpentier et ses Enfants*. On the clifftop is a war museum, particularly of the 1942 raid, with tanks, guns and military hardware.

Au Trou Normand, (35.84.59.84): old favourite of Dieppe visitors.
Classical cooking. Excellent fish. MEALS C–D. Shut Thursday.

PUTANGES-PONT-ECREPIN
[ORNE]

At the southern end of the Suisse-Normande on the willow-lined
Orne river this tiny, pleasant old market town is very popular
with French open-air holidaymakers. Once two towns, they were
joined by a mediaeval bridge which was destroyed in 1944 fighting and replaced with a modern one. New buildings are in stone
and traditional style, and there is a fine main square. Its market
along the river has been held for four hundred years. Few
foreign tourists have found it – a good hideout. 8km N is a
reservoir lake – Lac Rabodanges, where you can bathe,
windsurf, water-ski, picnic or take refreshment at a water's edge
restaurant. Nearby is Rabodanges Castle, 17th-century, in a
park.
   TOURIST INFORMATION Hôtel de Ville (33.35.02.44)

HOTEL
Lion Verd, place Hôtel de Ville (33.35.01.86): terrace by river
Orne; excellent value; good cooking with modern tendencies.
ROOMS A–D. MEALS A–E. Shut 1 December–10 January.

QUERQUEVILLE
[MANCHE]

Little seaside resort 5km NW Cherbourg. Small 6th to 8th-
centuries Chapel of St Germain; panoramic sea views.

QUIBERVILLE
[SEINE-MARITIME]

In a cove 16km W of Dieppe; rather untidy sand and gravel beach to which families come in mid-summer holidays, when it is lined with stalls selling most things from hamburgers to shellfish (known for mussels) and beach gear. Boats often sell fish direct on beach.

HOTEL
L'Huitrière (35.83.02.96): good modern Logis with pleasant dining room. Many bedrooms with balconies overlooking the sea. Excellent fish. ROOMS A–D. MEALS A–G (many menus). Shut 1 December–mid-January; Sunday evening, Friday in winter. Same family owns nearby Logis Les Falaises (35.83.04.03).

QUILLEBOEUF
[EURE]

Upstream on Seine from Tancarville Bridge. Once a Viking port, it was important until the 19th century. Now decaying since petrol installations were built at Port Jerome on opposite bank. Marais Vernier, land reclaimed in 1607 by Dutch engineers, not used for centuries, recently redrained with canals and reclaimed again. A lake and land around is a natural reserve for flowers and animals of the Marais and for Camargue horses and Scottish bulls. Ste Opportune-la-Mare beside the lake has an exhibition of apple varieties and cider production.

QUINEVILLE
[MANCHE]

Village on east Cotentin coast S of St Vaast-la-Hougue. Sand dunes. Sea views from cemetery. From here King James II wept as he saw his hope of regaining the English throne disappear in 1692 when an Anglo-Dutch fleet attacked the French ships of his invasion force and destroyed them in a four-day battle. Surprisingly grand château where James is said to have stayed, now a hotel beloved by the French.

HOTEL

Château de Quineville (33.21.42.67): bright and nicely furnished inside. Long lake with coarse fishing and terrace with good views. ROOMS D–E. MEALS B–E. Open 1 April–31 December; restaurant shut lunchtime 1 October–31 December.

RY
[SEINE-MARITIME]

In Crevon valley NW of Vascoeuil and the Lyons forest. Yonville-l'Abbaye of Flaubert's *Madame Bovary*. (A monument to Flaubert by the river.) Madame Bovary is said to have been based on Delphine Couturier, wife of a local doctor who died in 1848. It is the story of a respectable small town wife who became so bored she turned to vice for entertainment. Shops featured in this book still exist and an exhibition of mechanical figures in an old cider factory illustrates scenes from the story. (Open Monday, Saturday, Sunday; Easter–end October.) 4km SW is Château Martainville, a 15th-century brick and stone château with massive round towers and farm buildings (*see* page 168). 3km SE is Château de Vascoeuil, sturdy manor-house (14th to 16th centuries) in an ornamental French-style park. Rich interior. It is devoted to mementoes of French historian Jules Michelet (1798–1874).

RESTAURANT WITH ROOMS

Auberge La Crevonnière (35.23.60.52): romantic, pretty and peaceful, the river Crevon bubbling through the garden, willows shading garden tables. Inside – beams and friendliness. ROOMS (4 only) C. MEALS A–E. Shut 15 January–end February; Tuesday evening, Wednesday.

ST ANDRÉ-HÉBERTOT
[Calvados]

8½km from Pont-l'Évêque (page oo). Small village in lovely setting. Castle in an attractive park with ancient lime trees has a 1614 tower and 18th-century façade. Behind it is a 12th-century Romanesque church with a fine belfry.

ST AUBIN-SUR-MER
[Calvados]

Seaside resort 17km NW of Ouistreham said to be 'bracing'. Despite some damage in 1944, it is still a typical old-style French family holiday town.
TOURIST INFORMATION 1 rue Pasteur (31.97.30.47 – summer)

HOTEL
Clos Normand, Promenade Guynemer (31.97.30.41): facing sea, with terrace. ROOMS C–D. MEALS B–F. Open 24 March–20 October.

ST CHRISTOPHE-LE-JAJOLET
[Orne]

10km S of Argentan. The village church, dedicated to St Christopher, patron of travellers and sportsmen, is a centre for pilgrimages. On the last Sunday in July and the first Sunday in October, cars are driven to the monument to St Christopher outside the church to be blessed. Inside the church is a beautiful primitive Flemish painting *Burial of the Virgin*. Château de Sassy (18th and 19th centuries) stands near the village, built on three levels of terraces. Fine furniture, library and tapestries inside.

Magnificent gardens with a lake (open afternoons Whitsun–All Saints' Day).

ST JEAN-LE-THOMAS
[MANCHE]

Little seaside resort on north end of Mont-St-Michel Bay. Between here and Carolles from Pointe de Champeaux is the impressive view of Mont-St-Michel which General Eisenhower mentioned in his war memoirs. Attractive when the mimosa and wisteria are in bloom. Sands with good bathing, but the tide goes out for nearly a mile.

HOTEL

Bains (33.48.84.20): deservedly popular with British families for friendliness and excellent regional cooking. Some rooms in annexe. Swimming pool. ROOMS A–D. MEALS A–E. Open 20 March–10 October.

ST LAURENT-SUR-MER
[CALVADOS]

Just inland from Omaha Beach between Colleville and Vierville, it was captured by the Americans on the evening of D-Day. Nearby is the beautifully tended and impressive American Military Cemetery with 9386 graves. Just past it is the monument to the US 5th Engineer Special Brigade who did wonderful work clearing the beaches. South 5km at Surrain is a Museum of the Liberation.

ST LÔ
[MANCHE]

Poor St Lô received 4200 tons of Allied bombs in ninety minutes
in July 1944. With Caen, it was the worst hit town in Normandy
and was called Capital of the Ruins. The Germans had made it
the centre of their resistance to the American advance as Caen
was to the British advance. What was left of it fell to the Americans on 19 July. There's a monument in the rebuilt town to
Major Howie of the US Army. He wanted to be the first man to
enter the town. He was killed the day before. So men of his unit
carried his body into St Lô with them and put his coffin on the
ruins of the belfry of Ste Croix church. The reconstruction of St
Lô took twenty years and the modern concrete is hardly elegant.
The old upper part of the town, the mediaeval Enclos, is surrounded by a vast wall, partly rock, with tops of church and
houses peeping over it. Frankly the concrete modern tower
topped by a lion of the new town hall looks odd beside the
half-ruined old prison porch covered in ivy which is now dedicated to victims of the Nazis. What remained of the superb
church of Notre Dame has been saved, including two mutilated
towers. It was built in the 13th to 14th centuries and altered in
the 15th and 17th centuries. The green shale wall of the outside
has three beautiful modern bronze doors by Jean Bernard. The
outside pulpit is most unusual. There is a magnificent great
window by Max Ingrand in the chapel dedicated to St Thomas
of Canterbury.

The Musée de l'Hôtel de Ville holds but a shadow of the old St
Lô museum destroyed in the bombing but it does have eight
delightful 16th-century tapestries of lighthearted country scenes
called *The Loves of Gombaut and Macée*. The collection of 19th-
century paintings includes works by Millet, Corot, Rousseau and
a large, unusually colourful painting by Boudin, an artist not
known for strong colours. (Open daily except Tuesday July and
August, afternoons only September–July).

With the stud at Le Pin in Orne the Haras at St Lô is the most
important national stud in France. When they are all there, the
full complement is of nearly two hundred stallions. Most are

English or French thoroughbreds for breeding racehorses, French trotters, cobs and Percherons. (Visits lasting half-an-hour all year; guided mid-July–mid-February. At 10 a.m. on Thursday from the last Thursday in July to the first Thursday in September there are demonstrations of teams of horses.)

The river Vise is attractively lined with trees.

The French–American Memorial Hospital on D999 Villedieu road has a mosaic by Fernand Léger on one outside wall.

TOURIST INFORMATION 2 rue Havin (33.05.02.09)

MARKET Tuesday

HOTELS

Le Marignan, place de la Gare (33.05.15.15): good value. Comfortable rooms, good classic and regional cooking. Excellent wine list. ROOMS A–D. MEALS A–F. Shut part February.

Terminus, 3 ave Briovère (33.05.08.60): Logis. Rooms vary considerably. Cheap menus. Well run. ROOMS B–D. MEALS A–C. Shut 9 December–9 January. Hotel shut Saturday November–March but restaurant open.

ST MARTIN-DE-BOSCHERVILLE
[SEINE-MARITIME]

An abbey was founded here in 1050 by Raoul Tancarville, Grand Chamberlain to William the Conqueror. The large abbey church of St Georges which remains is a fine example of Norman Romanesque. The chapter house (12th century) has also survived.

ST PAIR-SUR-MER
[MANCHE]

Though only 3km from Granville, St Pair is quite different – very quiet with safe, golden sands backed by a breakwater promenade. Good for children. The church was founded in AD 540.

Of the original church there is one Romanesque bay beneath the belfry. The spire is 14th-century.

ST PIERRE-SUR-DIVES
[CALVADOS]

Lively little town on edge of Pays d'Auge makes most of the boxes for camembert cheese, and has many markets. Its 11th to 12th-century market hall, burnt down in 1944, has been rebuilt in the original style, using 290,000 chestnut pegs instead of screws or nails. Most impressive inside. The 13th-century lantern-tower of the old abbey church seen clearly above roof-tops is all that remains of a reconstructed abbey founded originally by William the Conqueror. Three modern stained-glass windows in the chancel tell the church's history. The town has a conservatory of cheese-making techniques.

6km S at Vendeuvre is an 18th–century château with an international museum of miniature furniture, old furnishings; collection of 18th-century smoking pipes. (Open afternoons 1 June–mid-September; Easter–31 May, mid-September–All Saints' Day Sunday afternoon only.)

TOURIST INFORMATION 17 rue St Benoît (31.90.81.68 – high season).

MARKET Monday

FESTIVAL Easter fair; dressage competition in June.

HOTELS

Gare et Restaurant Relais Fleurie, 47 boul. Collas (31.20.74.22): very cheap. ROOMS (simple) A. MEALS A–C.

Renaissance, 57 rue Lisieux (31.20.81.23): *Logis*. ROOMS A–D. MEALS A–B. Shut 15 September–10 October; restaurant shut Sunday.

ST SAUVEUR-LE-VICOMTE
[MANCHE]

Little town SW of Valognes on Cotentin Peninsula. Its great strong fortress was severely damaged in 1944 but retains two great towers flanking the entrance and a donjon. In the castle walls is built a retirement home. Through this and upstairs is a museum devoted to the novelist Jules Barbey d'Aurevilly (1808–89). Before the château entrance is a bronze bust of him by Rodin (daily except Tuesday July, August; afternoons only mid-June–July, 1–15 September, school holidays). Church (15th-century with 13th-century transept) contains works of art including a 15th-century statue of St James. A modern abbey with an 18th-century house is dedicated to Sainte Marie-Madeleine Postel, who founded an order in Cherbourg in 1807 and moved here in 1832.

ST SEVER-CALVADOS
[CALVADOS]

Large market town between Villedieu and Vire, named after 6th-century St Severus, a slave who converted his pagan master and founded an abbey here. The old abbey church (13th to 14th centuries) has 13th to 15th-century stained glass and a 17th-century freestanding belfry. Alongside is St Sever Forest, 1550 hectares of oak, beech, pine, fir.

MARKET St Sever, Saturday

ST VAAST-LA-HOUGUE
[MANCHE]

Delightful, small fishing port south of Barfleur on the NE coast of Cotentin Peninsula. Edward III of England landed his troops

here on their way to the famous victory at Crécy. Fortifications
were built in the 17th century after the English and Dutch had
defeated the French fleet off this coast, which was hoping to put
James II back on the throne of England. Locals call it St Va. Has
become popular with yachtsmen though at certain tides the
water goes out so far that it leaves tracts of muddy sand and
rocks. A fishermen's chapel on the quay is painted white to act as
a navigational mark. There is a long sand beach, Grande Plage, a
kilometre away on an isthmus which now joins St Vaast to the
former isle of La Hougue, which has a fort designed by Vauban.
The oyster beds in the bay produce some of the best oysters in
France. A fifteen minute walk north is Saire Point. From the top
of an old German *blockhaus* is a good view to St Vaast.

TOURIST INFORMATION quai Vauban (33.54.41.37 – 15
June–15 September).
MARKET Saturday

HOTEL
France et Fuchsias, rue Maréchal-Foch (33.54.42.26): delicious
little old-fashioned hotel covered in climbing fuchsias turning
the walls red when in bloom. Some bedrooms simple. Cooking is
delightful, many ingredients are from family farm; fish from
quayside. Must book in season. ROOMS B–E. MEALS A–F. Shut 3
January–1 March; Monday, Tuesday lunch low season.

ST VALÉRY-EN-CAUX
[SEINE-MARITIME]

Once a fishing port with boats sailing to the Arctic seas, it has
been turned into a very Norman little resort, its long harbour
bright with many pleasure boats. It is between Dieppe and
Fécamp. Like Étretat it stands between two cliffs, Falaises d'Aval
and d'Amont. Both are crowned with war memorials – one to
the 51st Highland Division, who fought a bloody rearguard
action here in 1940 to hold up German forces whilst the main
army escaped through Dunkirk. The Division was almost wiped

out. On the other cliff is a monument to the French 2nd Cavalry Division, who tried to fight Rommel's tanks with sabres. A third monument is to the airmen Coste and Bellonte, first to fly from Paris to New York in 1930.

St Valéry was rebuilt with foresight after wartime devastation. The new church built in 1963 in the market place is original and beautiful. A lofty wooden and glass building, with buttresses and beamed slate roof, it was designed by Lopez, with spectacular coloured glass walls by André Pierre Louis. The lovely Renaissance house (1540) with carved beams on the quayside, where Henri IV stayed, has been restored. Victor Hugo wrote a poem about St Valéry, 'Oh, Combien de Marins'. A few fishing boats have returned.

The population has been swollen by employees of the nearby Paluel nuclear power station at Conteville, 7km W.

TOURIST INFORMATION Tourist office, place Hôtel de Ville (35.97.00.63)

MARKETS Friday; also Sunday morning June–September

FESTIVALS Herring and cider fête in December

HOTELS

Terrasses, 22 rue Le Parrey (35.97.11.22): super situation beside the beach; comfortable, nice ambience. Good regional cooking of local products. Some bedrooms with sea view. ROOMS C–E. MEALS C–E. Shut 20 December-end February; Wednesday except July, August.

RESTAURANTS

Port (35.97.08.93): facing outer port. Pleasant atmosphere, reliable cooking; excellent fish. MEALS C–G. Shut 1–15 September; Thursday and Sunday evening; Monday.

Pigeon-Blanc, by old church (35.97.03.55): excellent value, loved by locals. MEALS A–E. Shut 15 December–15 January; Sunday evening low season; Thursday evening, Friday.

ST WANDRILLE
[SEINE-MARITIME *see* Caudebec-en-Caux, page 106]

STE MARGUERITE-SUR-MER
[SEINE-MARITIME]

12km W of Dieppe, a village-beach resort with pine woods and lovely gardens and villas on a walk to Vastérival. Some rare plants grow here. Ste Marguerite church is most unusual – Romanesque, with a 12th-century apse with interlaced arches, it has no transept. It was much remodelled in the 16th century but the rare high altar dates from 1160, plain, simple but lovely. The very colourful windows of the legend of Ste Marguerite are by Max Ingrand. The pebble beach under the cliffs can be dodgy for bathing and there is a steep walk back. Here and at Vastérival British commandos under Lord Lovat and Colonel Mills landed in the 1942 Dieppe raid, climbed through narrow gullies, destroyed German batteries and got away – the one complete success of the raid.

HOTEL
Sapins (35.85.11.45): simple, friendly, run by Grout family since 1888 and Britons stayed there then. ROOMS A–B. MEALS A–D. Open March–November.

STE MÈRE-ÉGLISE
[MANCHE]

Little town in the livestock breeding area of Normandy known for cattle and especially horses. At 2.30 a.m. on 6 June 1944 it was the scene of the first American invasion landing as General Ridgway's 82nd Airborne Division virtually used it as an airfield to bring in parachutists and gliders. They took the town but a fierce German counter-attack led to bloody fighting until tanks landed on Utah Beach arrived on 7 June. The 13th-century church was damaged by Americans dislodging German machine-gunners from its belfry. Modern glass on the door records the action. There is a monument in the square and 'Milestone O' outside the town hall – first of the symbolic milestones recording the US Army's advance to Metz and Bastogne. An Airborne Troops museum (including a Douglas dropping plane) is open every day March–mid-November; Saturday and Sunday only; except mid-November–mid-December; shut mid-December–end February. An interesting farm museum in the garden and buildings of the 16th-century Beauvais farm shows implements, machinery and domestic items of peasant life of 80–100 years ago. (Open every day July and August. Easter–end of June and September shut Tuesday; October open Saturday, Sunday afternoon; shut November–Easter).

STE-MARIE-DU-MONT
[MANCHE]

On D913 road from Utah Beach (once called Dunes de Varreville) towards Carentan, a village with a most impressive Church of St Mary. You see first the square 14th-century tower with a Renaissance top storey. But the church is basically Romanesque 12th-century with 14th-century transept and chancel. There is a Utah Beach Landing Museum here and a monument to 800 Danish sailors who took part in the landing.

SÉES
[ORNE]

Charming, quiet ancient cathedral city which seems to live in past centuries. Its streets are rich in old houses, some rather faded. The two sixty metre spires of the cathedral of St Latrium's dominate the city and can be seen for miles around – sometimes just a tantalising glimpse over ridges.

The bishopric of Sées was old when Norsemen marauders came and destroyed the old cathedral. Centuries later, when the Norsemen had settled and become Norman and Christian reparation was made and they built the 12th to 13th-century Norman–Gothic cathedral. The chancel with columns climbing to a vaulted roof is lit by vast windows, some still with the rich colouring of 13th-century craftsmen. The 14th-century marble Madonna and Child facing the high altar is very beautiful.

The cathedral is in a pleasant market square. There's a Son-et-Lumière in mid-summer. Alas, some other fine old buildings are closed to the public (Abbey of St Martin, Bishop's Palace – Ancient Évêché) and you can only see the 13th-century Notre-Dame-de-la-Place church by seeking the key from the caretaker. But they are all worth seeing from the outside. Écouves Forest (page 128) starts only 6km away; Château d'O (page 173) is 7km W.

TOURIST INFORMATION Hôtel de Ville (April–end September – 33.28.74.79)

MARKET Saturday

HOTELS

Cheval Blanc, 1 place St-Pierre (33.27.80.48): delightful simple and pretty black and white country inn. Country cooking. ROOMS A–B. MEALS A–F. Shut mid-October–early November, 1–15 February; Thursday evening, Friday in summer, Friday evening, Saturday low season.

Ile de Sées, at Macé, 5km N158, D303 (33.27.98.65): converted creeper-clad dairy; very comfortable; big garden; quiet. ROOMS C–D. MEALS B–E. Shut 15 December–15 January; Sunday evening, Monday.

TANCARVILLE
[SEINE-MARITIME]

Known now for its great road bridge which altered the map of North France. Until 1959 there was no bridge across the Seine between Le Havre and Rouen (a stretch of 125km). Little ferries (*bac*) crossed but could not take many vehicles or big loads. The bridge is 1400 metre long. There is a toll. It revitalised towns on both sides of the Seine. The old village of Tancarville is below the bridge and ruins of a castle built by Henry I of England remain on a spur, from which there are spectacular views of the Seine's right bank. The Eagle tower of the castle remains. The 18th-century Château-Neuf is nearby.

HOTEL

Marine (35.39.77.15): old ferry inn of pre-bridge days has attractive lawns and gardens by the river. ROOMS C–E. MEALS C–F. Shut mid-July–mid-August, part February; Sunday evening, Monday.

TESSÉ-LA-MADELEINE
[ORNE – *see* Bagnoles-de-l'Orne, page 80]

THURY-HARCOURT
[CALVADOS]

Popular resort on north edge of Suisse-Normande, base for exploring the Orne river and countryside. A circuit of typical country and villages is marked by signposts. The town was rebuilt after nearly complete destruction in 1944, but the Château of the Dukes of Harcourt was burned to the ground and the ruins have been left, the grounds made into a public park. Nearby the Orne river loops spectacularly through cliffs (Boucle du Hom). To reach it, take D6 from Thury-Harcourt then D212 by the river bank. This skirts the river.

TOURIST INFORMATION Tourist Office, place St Saveur
(31.79.70.45)

HOTELS

Poste, boul. du 30-Juin (31.79.72.12): old Relais in magnificent

gardens. Fresh local ingredients simply but very nicely cooked.
ROOMS C–E. MEALS C–F. Shut January, February.
Auberge du Pont de Brie, at Goupillières, 8km by D6, D212, 1km
on D171 – Halte de Grimbosq (31.79.37.84): woman chef produces meals of 'harmonious balance between tradition and
originality'. Quiet, attractive hotel. ROOMS B–C. MEALS B–D.
Shut Wendesday except July, August.

TORIGNI-SUR-VIRE
[MANCHE]

15km SE of St Lô on N174. A vast, good-looking 16th-century
Matignon-family castle has been faithfully reconstructed and
restored after 1944 destruction. Its east wing has fine Louis
XIII, Louis XIV and Louis XVI furniture and beautiful tapestries of Brussels and Aubusson. It is in parkland with shady
trees, walks and boating lakes. One of the Matignon family
married a Grimaldi and became a Prince of Monaco. (Castle
open afternoons except Sunday 1 April–end September.)

TOUQUES
[CALVADOS]

On the Touques river just inland from Deauville it was the port
from which William the Conqueror's son William Rufus sailed to
take up the English crown. The foundation stone of the church
of St Thomas was laid by Thomas à Becket. Some charming old
houses along the river. The Rothschild stud for breeding racehorses is at the 16th-century Manoir de Méautry.

RESTAURANTS
Relais du Haras, 23 rue Louvel-et-Brières (31.88.43.98): where
the horsey set meet. Excellent meals, but pricey. MEALS E–G.
Shut 15–31 January, 25 June–5 July.

Landiers, 90 rue Louvel-et-Brières (31.88.00.39): Norman relais, excellent lower-price menu. MEALS C–F. Shut Tuesday evening, Wednesday.

TOUROUVRE
[ORNE]

12km NE of Mortagne-au-Perche, pleasant little town on edge of Perche Forest, good walking centre. The church has a 15th-century painting of the Adoration of the Magi incorporated into its 17th-century altarpiece. Two stained-glass windows show local families leaving for the foundation of Québec. (Church shut on Monday.)

TOURIST INFORMATION beside the church
(33.25.74.55)

HOTEL

France, 19 rue du 14-Août 1944 (33.25.73.55): Logis. Good value. ROOMS A–E. MEALS A–E. Shut 15 December–5 January; Sunday evening, Monday (September–June).

TRELLY
[MANCHE]

A tiny village 13km south of Coutances by D971 in the very heart of the Manche countryside – the true bocage where steep banks are almost completely covered in spring by primroses, then cowslips. Little signs marked 'Verte Campagne' take you through a maze of lanes to the hamlet of Chevalier and a low grey stone farmhouse built in 1717, with roses climbing it, green verges and flower beds leading to meadows, chickens clucking in the outbuildings. It is the home of Madame Meredith, widow of a Royal Navy officer, and is now a loveable little hotel – total haven of peace.

HOTEL

Verte Campagne (33.47.65.33): relaxed, charming, friendly. Some bedrooms small. Cooking traditional, good. ROOMS B–E. MEALS A–F. Shut 15–30 January, mid-November–early December; Sunday evening, Monday in winter.

LE TRÉPORT
[SEINE-MARITIME]

A delightful old-fashioned little fishing port and resort which is lively and happy in mid-summer, as if it is always *en fête*. It has always lured Parisians. Right on the borders of Normandy and Picardy, 30km NE of Dieppe, at the mouth of the little river Bresle, it is only 171km from Paris and Eu is only 5km inland. Across the river is its twin town of Les-Mers-les-Bains, which is really its quieter suburb, but is in the Somme *Département*. The long shingle beach is backed by tall cliffs reached by chair-lift from the town, with fine coastal views from the top terrace.

Tréport used to be as important as Dieppe as a port until the river was diverted and silted up. When Louis-Philippe was king last century, with his favourite palace at Eu, Tréport became very fashionable indeed. Parisians flocked there to be near the Royal Court. Queen Victoria liked it and wrote about it. For its resistance in the Second World War, when it suffered severe damage, the town was awarded the Croix de Guerre. The tall white cliffs give this stretch of coast down to Le Havre the name of the Alabaster Coast. Shops and fish restaurants line the harbour quay and the promenade stretches to the white lighthouse. There's a casino.

TOURIST INFORMATION Tourist Office, Esplanade
Plage 35.86.06.69 (shut Tuesday, Sunday)

HOTELS

Picardie, place P. Sémard (35.86.02.22): ROOMS B–E. MEALS C–G. Shut 6 December–20 January; Sunday evening, Monday in winter.
Bellevue, at Mers-les-Bains – esplanade Général-Leclerc

(35.86.12.89): 30 metres from sea; cheap, good value. ROOMS A–C. MEALS A–C. Open all year.

TROUVILLE
[CALVADOS]

Trouville was fashionable when its neighbour Deauville was a tiny farming hamlet. A fishing village, it drew the rich and famous last century when a casino was built there. But the casino rent was put up, the casino moved to the smaller hamlet across the river. Top people went to Deauville, their servants and the middle-classes went to Trouville. Deauville still looks down on it. It is certainly cheaper. It has a fine sand beach, fair nightlife, a Napoleon III style casino and a very large open-air swimming pool. Like Deauville, it has Les Planches, the wooden board walk stretching the whole of its beach. It still has some of the atmosphere of a fishing village, with fishing boats moored up river and a Norman-style fish market.

The combination of light and space, sea and sky and the long view to Le Havre headland lured the Impressionist painters and in the Musée Montebello are works of Boudin, and Jongkind, as well as the miniaturist Isaby, Dufy, Mozin (whose work made Trouville popular in Paris) and others (open Saturday, Sunday afternoon Easter–15 June; all afternoons except Tuesday in summer). The aquarium has sea and freshwater fish and marine reptiles in near-natural surrounds (open daily in summer, afternoons rest of year).

From the Corniche beside boulevard Briand are superb views of the beaches of Trouville and Deauville and of the Côte Fleurie, the charming 19km of coast down to Cabourg. The coast road the other way, 19km to Honfleur called Corniche Normande, passes magnificent scenery and seascapes, with snatched views of the Seine Estuary through orchards. Traffic is formidable in mid-summer.

TOURIST INFORMATION Tourist Office, 32 boul. F. Moureux (31.88.36.19)
MARKETS Wednesday, Sunday; daily Easter–September

HOTELS

Carmen, 24 rue Carnot (31.88.35.43): pleasant Logis about 300 metres from beach. ROOMS B–E. MEALS A–D. Shut 4 January–8 February; 18–27 April; 16–24 October. Restaurant shut Monday evening, Tuesday except mid-summer.

L'Amiénoise, 5 rue Bon-Secours (31.88.12.23): old-style French seaside hotel. Quiet street. No restaurant. ROOMS C–D. Shut 15 November–15 February.

RESTAURANTS

Galetée Bar, on beach (31.88.15.04): away from petrol fumes. Splendid fish freshly cooked. Friendly, popular. MEALS D–E. Shut mid-November–1 April; Thursday except July–August.

Roches-Noires, 16 boul. Louis-Bréguet (31.88.12.19): named after a long-gone hotel where the famous stayed. Small, run by Ducroux family who had a much-liked Paris restaurant. Madame is a well-known chef – fine straightforward cooking with regional slant. MEALS F–G. Shut mid-January to mid-February; Tuesday, Wednesday low season.

Les Vapeurs, 160 boul. Fernand-Moureux (31.88.15.24): a 1930s style bistro with old posters, mirrors and waiters dressed in black trousers and waistcoats; fashionable for over thirty years. Fish cooked to your order. Open into small hours. Lively, noisy, busy and fun. Ignored by Michelin. MEALS E–G. Shut 4.30 January, two weeks at end November; Tuesday evening, Wednesday in winter.

VALOGNES
[MANCHE]

In the 18th century they called Valognes, SE of Cherbourg, 'the Versailles of Normandy'. All that changed during the American advance in 1944 when the town was nearly wiped out. It was rebuilt in concrete. Some 17th- and 18th-century houses have been restored. Hôtel de Beaumont is worth seeing, if only for its noble façade overlooking a terrace garden, for it is 50 metres long. It was the setting for a novel by Barbey d'Aurevilly, who lived in the town. It is richly furnished (open afternoons 1

July–mid-September). The majestic 17th to 18th-century Château de Siminane is now the town hall. An interesting cider museum (Musée Régional du Cidre) traces the history of apple growing and cider making. It is in an attractive 15th-century Logis. (Open mid-June–end September except Wednesday). A museum of eau-de-vie (distilled spirits) is in the 17th-century Hôtel de Thieuville (open as cider museum).

Now Valognes is known for butter-making. Though dull-looking, it is quite a lively and likeable little place, especially on market days. 8½km NW of Volognes are the ruins of the castle of Brix, ancestral home of the Bruce (de Bruis) family, one of whom invaded England with William the Conqueror. His descendant, Robert the Bruce, became King of Scotland and victor of the battle of Bannockburn.

TOURIST INFORMATION Syndicat, place Château
(33.40.11.55)
MARKET Tuesday, Friday

HOTELS

Louvre, 28 rue Réligieuses (33.40.00.07): renowned locally for remarkable value. Simone Mesnil's cooking is straightforward and excellent. Rooms vary. ROOMS A–C. MEALS A–C. Shut 1 December–5 January. Restaurant shut Saturday low season.

Agriculture, 16 rue Léopold-Delisle (33.95.02.02): Logis with trenchermen's meals. ROOMS A–C. MEALS A–D. Restaurant shut Sunday evening except in July, August (Monday).

VARENGEVILLE-SUR-MER
[SEINE-MARITIME]

Delightful village 5km W of Dieppe which has always attracted painters. Its houses hide in groups among trees along sunken bocage roads. Three gorges lead down to the sea. The church is so dramatically near the cliff edge that it had to be saved recently from collapse. Mostly 14th century, it still has 12th-century Romanesque features and a beautiful Tree of Jesse window by Georges Braque, originator, with Picasso of Cubism. He lived nearby and his grave recording his death in 1963 is in the churchyard, with a tomb decorated by his pupils with the blue bird messenger design of his paintings. The other decorative window in the church is by Raoul Ubac. The musician Albert Roussel is buried here, too.

More of Braque's superb windows are in nearby Chapelle Saint-Dominique. Monet lived in Varengeville when he was poor and his painting of the church is in the Barber Institute in Birmingham (England).

Parc des Moustiers is a superb garden around a house designed in 1898 by Sir Edward Lutyens (1869–1944), the architect of New Delhi in India. The great turn-of-the-century landscape gardener, Gertude Jekyll, laid out the gardens in English style with sweeping lawns and magnificently coloured massed shrubs, especially azaleas, and rare camellias, paths and alleys leading to beds of rare plants, roses, hydrangeas, rhododendrons and rare clematis. The musician Guillaume Mallet carried on the work for forty years, introducing trees from around the world (gardens open daily 15 March–15 November, April–June are best months for colour; house open by appointment –phone 35.85.10.02).

On the village edge a narrow avenue of beeches leads to Manoir d'Ango, a delightful Florentine-style Renaissance mansion built by Jean Ango, Dieppe shipbuilder whose corsair fleet preyed on rich merchantmen, especially Portuguese, and made him rich enough to become moneylender to François I (*see* Dieppe page 23). Built in black and white stones around a quadrangle, and steep roofed, it has raised arch galleries topped by a frieze with the monogram of François, who often stayed there. The dovecote is vast. A round tower with an Oriental dome, it housed 1600 pairs of doves. Ango went bankrupt because François, who spent fortunes on wars, ostentatious living and châteaux building, was bankrupt himself and could not repay Ango. (Visits to see exterior daily, end March–early November; Saturday and Sunday in winter).

Terrasse, 3km NW at Vastérival (35.85.12.54): Delafontaine family here since 1911. Friendly old French family hotel with French family cooking. Lovely country position high above sea with views. Very reasonable prices. ROOMS B–E. MEALS A–E. Shut 15 October–16 March.

VASCOEUIL
[EURE]

The red-brick château (14th–16th centuries) is a cultural centre, devoted largely to the historian Jules Michelet (1798–1874), who lived here and wrote his 24–volume *Histoire de France* and 7-volume *Histoire de la Révolution*. The château is 9km NW of Lyons-la-Forêt where the Crevon river meets the Andelle. It is used for modern art exhibitions. Its courtyard is decorated with sculptures and mosaics by Braque, Salvador Dali, Vasarely and Folon, and beyond is a lovely 17th-century dovecote. In the gardens and park Michelet built old-style Norman cottages, half timbered and thatched (open afternoons Easter–All Saints' Day).

VAUVILLE
[MANCHE]

A charming hamlet 7km S of Beaumont on the west coast of the Cotentin in a hollow among high sand dunes on a wild bay. The country church and Renaissance manor house are very attrac-

tive. From a steep hill by the next village of Le Petit-Thot there
are magnificent views of the bay (Anse de Vauville) and the
windswept heaths behind. Camp Maneyrol has long been used
for gliding. 4km S is another spot for enormous panoramic
views – Calvaire des Dunes at Biville, from which you can sometimes see the Channel Isles. The interesting little 12th to 14th-
century church has a window by Barillet showing the 1944
Liberation.

VERNEUIL-SUR-AVRE
[EURE]

An excellent centre to stay for a day or two. Rich in architectural
and artistic treasures, it also has two delightful hotel-restaurants.
It was founded by Henry I of England right on Normandy's
southern border to link with frontier forts at Tillières and Non-
ancourt to keep out the French. In 1424, during the Hundred
Years War, Charles VII failed to take it with a large force which
included 5000 Scottish archers and 2000 wild Highland axe-
men. It fell to the French 25 years later through traitors in the
Anglo-Norman camp. The river Iton still laps the old walls.

Its big open market place, colourful during Saturday markets, is dominated by the superb Flamboyant tower of La
Madeleine church, described as a 'mediaeval skyscraper'. It has
been likened to Rouen's Butter Tower, and it looks rather similar with three tiers of arches and stone tracery, niches with
twenty-four beautiful statues, all topped by a graceful octagonal
lantern. The church itself, rather sloppily restored last century,
contains some fine 16th-century and earlier stautes.

The red-brick 12th-century church of Notre Dame has been
much altered over centuries but has interesting statues from
different periods. The wooden polychrome 13th-century Virgin
is beautiful. St Christopher is huge and St Denis is holding onto
his head which had been severed by the executioner (open only
Saturday, Sunday). The circular redstone Tour Grise remains
from Henry's castle, and there are old houses (15th to 16th
centuries).

HOTELS

Hostellerie du Clos, 98 rue Ferté-Vidame (32.32.21.81): *Grande
Epoque* manor house where Patrick Simon cooks superbly and
delicately in traditional style. Superb fish. Elegant, very comfortable rooms. Charming flowered terrace. Relais et Châteaux
hotel. Rooms F–G. Meals G. Shut December, January; Monday
(except hotel in season).

Saumon, 89 place Madeleine (32.32.02.36): outstanding value.
Old coaching inn run by son of Patrick Simon (Le Clos). Tradi-
tional Norman hearty meals. Rooms modernised. Rooms A–D.
Meals A–D. Shut 24 December–6 January.

VERNON
[Eure]

Pleasant town on the Seine with fine avenues and a useful
modern bridge. Parisians go here for days out or weekends.
Seine barges call.

It was created by Rollo, first Duke of Normandy, in the 9th
century. From the bridge you can see beyond wooded islands to
Vernonett on the opposite bank, beginning of Vernon Forest.
Here are remains of the castle built by Henry I of England to
protect his wooden bridge below. The wooden piles of his bridge
can still be seen. He built another fortress across the river. Its
keep, Archives Tower, is still there, much restored. Notre Dame
church was built between the 11th and 17th centuries with
several styles. It has fine 17th-century tapestries and beautiful
stained glass, especially a rose window, and a lovely 18th-century
high altar.

2km SW by D181 is Château de Bizy, built in 1740 and
reconstructed in Italian palazzo style in the 19th century, set in a
beautiful wooded park with waterfalls, it still has an attractive

18th-century courtyard and outbuildings. Inside are mementoes of Napoleon and other military commanders. A collection of old cars is in the stables. The château belongs to the Duke of Albuféra. The park was laid out for a previous owner, King Louis-Philippe (open every day except Fridays 1 April–31 October). Poulain Municipal Museum includes two paintings by Monet (closed Monday). Monet's house at Giverny is 4km away.

TOURIST INFORMATION Syndicat d'Initiative, passage Pasteur (32.51.39.60)

HOTELS

Evreux et Relais Normand, 11 place d'Evreux (32.51.16.12): 18th-century hotel. Good cooking. ROOMS C–E. MEALS C–D. Restaurant shut August; Monday.

RESTAURANT

Beau Rivage, 13 ave Maréchal-Leclerc (32.51.17.27): classical, straightforward cooking using local products. MEALS C–F. Shut 1–15 February; 1–15 October; Sunday evening, Monday.

VER-SUR-MER
[CALVADOS]

The spearhead of the British 50th Division (Northumberlands) landed at this little seaside resort at 7.25 a.m. on D-Day and fought their way along the coast to take Arromanches (Gold Beach). A monument stands in the main street – avenue du Colonel Harper. (*see* D-Day Beaches page 57). A massive 11th-century Romanesque church tower survived. This is a camping and caravanning stretch of coast.

VEULES-LES-ROSES
[SEINE-MARITIME]

Once a little port between Dieppe and St Valéry-en-Caux, this is now a delightful little seaside resort, hidden between high wooded cliffs. Its pretty main street is rich in roses in summer. La Veule, a tiny river, ripples through the town with an occasional flash of trout. Beside a pebble beach are restaurants, a small casino, a little entertainment and a children's club in season. Off season it sleeps. Its 16th-century church has a 13th-century lantern and ancient statues. A VVF (family summer holiday centre) opened recently. In the 1830s onwards it was fashionable with Parisian actors and actresses and authors.

RESTAURANT
Les Galets (35.97.61.33): terrace overlooking the beach. Magnificent cooking by Gilbert Plaisance, very much his own man – Norman cooking neither classic nor nouvelle dishes but inventive, superb pâtisseries. Pricey. Book. MEALS F–G. Shut February; Tuesday evening, Wednesday.

VEULETTES-SUR-MER
[SEINE-MARITIME]

Little beach resort 10km W of St Valéry-en-Caux, in a wide, green valley of the Durdent has found itself recently with Le Paluel nuclear station as a neighbour. Perhaps it is the continued wrath of God. Once there was a city called Grande Ville de Durdent here, fishermen say. But its ways were so evil that even St Valery failed to purify it. So he sought the wrath of the Almighty, who called the waves to inundate it. Fishermen say that they can still see it sometimes under the water. Veulettes has a casino (open Easter–end October), a disco and even miniature golf but it also has an 11th-century church with a lantern tower. And it's a family resort.

HOTEL WITH RESTAURANT
Les Frégates (35.97.51.22): Logis, facing the sea. Enclosed terrace. ROOMS C. MEALS B–E. Restaurant only shut 21 December–4 January; Sunday evening, Monday lunch.

VIERVILLE-SUR-MER
[CALVADOS]

Little resort on Omaha Beach where Americans landed on D-Day. Exhibition '6 June 1944' (open daily April–September). Memorial on German *blockhaus* to American National Guard.

VILLEDIEU-LES-POÊLES
[MANCHE]

Delightfully animated little town east of Granville in the Seine valley. Its strange name – God's Town of the Frying Pans – grew from its history, first as a Commandery of the Knights of St John of Jerusalem in the 12th century, then from the 17th century as the town producing the best copper pans in France, which it still does. Once it made also the round-bellied copper milk *cannes* for every Norman farm. It has a bell foundry which you can visit (open daily except Sunday and Monday in winter), and workshop and museum of leatherwork and 'point de Villedieu' lace (workshop open daily except Sunday and Monday low season; museum open early June–mid-September). Inevitably there is also a most interesting workshop and museum of copperware (open all year). Little workshops are hidden away in alleys and courtyards with names like 'Court of Hell, Court of the Lilies, Court of the Three Kings, Monks Court', and old houses line the river banks. Its 18th-century Flamboyant church, which replaced the Knights' church, has a square tower ornamented with heraldic emblems of the Knights. Every four years since 1655 there has been a procession to the church called Grand-Sacré (Great Coronation) of members of the Order of St John

(1991, 1995 etc. 2nd or 3rd Sunday in June). But Villedieu is by no means a fusty old town living in its past. It is a shopping centre for a wide area, with lively little individual shops, and the centre of a prosperous cattle-raising area with a crowded Tuesday market.

Champrépus Zoo, 8km along D924 Granville road, has eighty different species, kept in semi-freedom, from monkeys and kangaroos to bears and tigers. Attractive gardens.

TOURIST INFORMATION Tourist Office, place Costils (June–September 33.61.05.69) Hôtel de Ville (rest of year – 33.61.00.16)

MARKET Tuesday

FESTIVAL See above

HOTELS

St Pierre-et-St-Michel, 12 place République (33.61.00.11): genuine old-style Norman hotel used by locals. Very good value. Bourgeois cooking of local products, generous portions. Bedrooms renovated. Steep stairs. ROOMS A–D. MEALS A–D. Shut 26 December–mid-January; Friday in winter.

Le Fruitier, rue Général-de-Gaulle (33.51.14.24): renovated, extended, improved. ROOMS B–D. MEALS A–C. Shut 15–28 February.

Manoir de l'Acherie, 4km E by D554 (33.51.13.87): old manor restored.Old-style cooking, good sauces. Good value. Old-style ROOMS E. MEALS A–E. Shut 27 June–11 July; Monday (except hotel in July, August).

VILLEQUIER
[SEINE-MARITIME]

Small village on right bank of the Seine down stream from Caudebec and Brotonne bridge, below wooded foothills. Here in 1843 Victor Hugo's daughter Léopoldine and her husband Charles Vacquerie were drowned by the huge Seine tidal bore, which has since been tamed by locks. The couple's grave is in the village churchyard, with Hugo's wife Adèle. Hugo wrote a poem called 'Contemplations' about his grief. There is a Victor Hugo museum in the old house which belonged to Charles Vacquerie's family, manufacturers from Le Havre (shut Tuesday, and Monday in winter). Just outside the village towards Caudebec is a 15th-century manor, Maison Blanche, with a tower. The restored cellar and ground floor are used for art exhibitions from early July to mid-August. The fine, old Château de Villequier on a hill with superb panoramic views was restored after damage by fire in 1763. Complete with fine, domed dovecote, Louis XIII stables and miniature Petit Trianon, it was turned into a magnificent luxury hotel which, alas, has now failed financially.

HOTELS

Grand Sapin (35.56.78.73): old-fashioned hotel with terrace onto the Seine and good old-style bourgeoise cuisine. Good fish. Same chef-patron for very many years; very simple rooms and plumbing. ROOMS A–B. MEALS A–E. Shut 15 January–5 February, 15–30 November; Tuesday evening, Wednesday off season.

VILLERS-BOCAGE
[CALVADOS]

A 'new' town, completely rebuilt after 1944 bombardment, on the edge of the Bocage Normand, on N175, 26km SW of Caen. Its modern buildings are architecturally interesting, especially the covered market with a huge flat roof supported by slim ironwork pillars, and St Martin's Church in stone and concrete with pleasant interior. Lively Wednesday cattle market.

HOTEL

Les Trois Rois, route Vire (31.77.00.32): master-chef Henri Martinotti is famous for his tripe but his stuffed turbot and *chausson* of lobster (in pastry) are nicer. Outstanding imaginative cooking. Logis. ROOMS C–E. MEALS C–F. Shut 1–20 February, 26 June–3 July.

VILLERS-SUR-MER
[CALVADOS]

An elegant, convenient resort on the Côte Fleurie 8km SW of Deauville, little known outside of France. Grouped on a wooded hillside at the end of a 5km sandy beach, it has nice restaurants and bars, good shops and attractive wooded countryside behind it. Quite lively in season. The beach slopes gently – good for children. An hour's walk along the beach at low tide or by D163 and footpath are the Vaches Noires cliffs, crumbling, hollowed out, with many fossils (*see also* Houlgate).

TOURIST INFORMATION Tourist Office, place Mermoz (31.87.01.18)

HOTELS

Relais du Manoir, chemin Manoir d'Auberville (31.87.45.60): extremely comfortable. ROOMS F–G. MEALS D–G. Open all year.
Bonne Auberge, rue Maréchal-Leclerc (31.87.04.64): very comfortable. ROOMS E–F. MEALS D–E. Shut 1 December–15 February.

VILLERVILLE
[CALVADOS]

Little resort on Corniche Normande between Trouville and Honfleur. Country setting among trees. Lively in summer. View from terrace above the beach to Le Havre. At low tide the Ratier rocks are exposed and mussel gatherers move in.

HOTEL

Manoir du Grand Bec (31.88.09.88): ROOMS D–F. MEALS D–F. Open all year.

VIMOUTIERS
[ORNE]

Very pleasant little town south of Lisieux, 3km north of Camembert (*see* page 101). Here the Camembert farmer's wife Marie Harel first marketed her cheese in 1970. Her statue in the huge main square was gratefully donated by an American cheese importing company. Still a big cheese and butter centre with a camembert museum at 10 avenue Général-de-Gaulle – showing farm cheese-making with tastings (open daily except Monday morning 1 April–31 October; except Saturday morning, Sunday, Monday morning in winter).

Hills and valleys surrounding the town produce cider apples and calvados is distilled in Vimoutiers. You can see it made and taste it at Anée, 27 rue du Perré Monday–Friday. Apple Fair is held for three days in mid-October and a local society is called Les Chevaliers du Trou Normand (the Trou Normand is a glass of calvados swallowed as a *digestif* during a meal to make a hole – *trou* – for more food).

There's a fine church by river Vie. At the entrance to town is an unusual Allied war memorial – a German Tiger tank knocked out by the Canadians in the Falaise Gap fighting in 1944.

TOURIST INFORMATION Tourist Office, 10 ave
Général-de-Gaulle (33.39.30.29)
MARKET Monday afternoon
FESTIVAL Appel Fair mid-October

HOTELS

L'Escale du Vitou, route d'Argentan, 2km by D916 (33.39.12.04): Logis de France which is also an open-air leisure centre (big pool, grass skiing, fishing, pedaloes on lake, etc). Rooms in bungalows. Good restaurant (33.39.12.37). ROOMS C–D. MEALS A–D. Hotel open all year. Restaurant shut January; Sunday evening, Monday.

VIRE
[CALVADOS]

Poor Vire, standing proudly on an escarpment at an important
road junction between Brittany and eastern Normandy above
the rolling Norman countryside, was inevitably almost
annihilated in 1944. A fortress town since the 8th century, it was
strengthened in the 12th century by Henry I of England who
built a castle. Richelieu knocked it down in 1630. Part of two
towers remain. The delightful but not pretty 15th-century belfry
on top of the 13th-century gate, Tour de L'Horloge, has survived and is still the chief entrance to the main square. The
Gothic 13th to 15th-century church has been restored. The
museum in the old Hôtel Dieu has some interesting modern
sculptures of birds by Anne Marie Profillet (1898–1939). In the
grounds is a reconstructed Norman farmhouse (open daily
except Tuesday 1 May–30 September, then afternoons).

The surrounding scenery is enchanting – the Vire river,
forests, deep ravines, cottages, old manor houses. There are
good views of the meeting of the Vire and Virenne rivers from
Rocher des Rames viewpoint, south-west of the town. The two
valleys are called Vaux de Vire, and this name was given to songs
which once made Vire famous. Olivier Basselin made up these
bawdy tavern drinking songs called Vaux de Vire for the cloth-
iers in the 14th century; they spread far beyond Vire and the
name became corrupted to Vaudeville. Now Vire is known for
its *andouilles* – large sausages made of pork chitterlings. Vire
andouilles are smoked over oak wood until black and marbly –
usually served sliced and cold as a first course.

TOURIST INFORMATION Tourist Office, square
Résistance (31.68.00.05)
MARKET Friday

HOTELS

Cheval Blanc, 2 place du 6 Juin-1944 (31.68.00.21): young chef
has taken over after a bad patch and improved cooking and
atmosphere. Traditional Norman cooking lightened. ROOMS

B–E. MEALS B–F. Shut 20 December–20 January; Friday evening, Saturday lunch low season.

Manoir de la Pommeraie, at Roulloirs, 3km SE on D524 (31.68.07.71): well-known Norman chef Georges Lesage has moved to an elegant 18th-century country manor in pretty grounds. Cheapest menu is splendid value. Refined traditional cooking. MEALS C–G. Shut part February; Sunday evening, Wednesday.

YPORT
[SEINE-MARITIME]

Very pleasant little old-style seaside resort SW of Fécamp, where a few families still fish. Its pebble beach where the boats rest nestles under white cliffs used on tourist posters. Maupassant wrote *Une Vie* here, Jean Lorrain wrote *Très Russe* and a local painter Jef Friboulet gave the church very original paintings of five stations of the Cross. Yport sleeps in winter.

HOTEL
La Sirène, boul. Alexandre-Dumont (35.27.31.87): nice little hotel on the front. Good cooking, several menus. ROOMS B–C. MEALS A–E.

YVETOT
[SEINE-MARITIME]

Lively market town on the Caux plateau. Shopping and business centre for the Durdent valley villages and farms. Almost wiped out in 1940 bombing, it has been pleasantly rebuilt with a spectacular round church in concrete and glass by architect Yves Marchand (1956). To one side a tall slender bell-tower rises to 30 metres. A massive panel above the centre door shows St Peter standing against a gigantic fisherman's net reaching to the roof. Inside, the huge wall of stained glass by Max Ingrand showing the lives of Norman saints and the Crucifixion is absolutely magnificent. The impact of the colours is truly dazzling – blue turning to purple and vivid red, brilliant backgrounds of gold and yellow, the red Crucifixion with the simple deep blue of Mary's gown encircled in blue. This is surely some of the greatest coloured glass conceived through the centuries.

Yvetot had Viking origins, linked to Yvetofta on Lake Ivo in Sweden. It was a legendary 'kingdom' of old songs, because from 1392 to the Revolution it was an independent territory where the local lord was called 'king'. In the 19th century the celebrated *chansonnier* Béranger wrote a song of Yvetot's king who 'got up late, slept too much and well'. When Henri IV freed the town from the Catholic League forces, he said: 'If by bad luck I lose the crown of France, I am sure to have the crown of Yvetot'.

TOURIST INFORMATION Syndicat d'Initiative
(35.95.08.40–April–September)
MARKET Wednesday morning

HOTEL

Havre, place des Belges (35.95.16.77): pleasant, busy commercial hotel in centre. ROOMS C–E. MEALS B–D. Restaurant shut 17 December–16 January; Friday evening except July, August, Sunday.

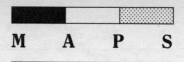

M A P S

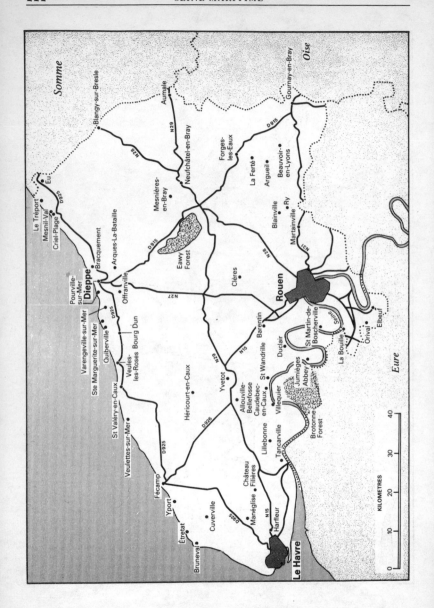

3   *Seine-Maritime*

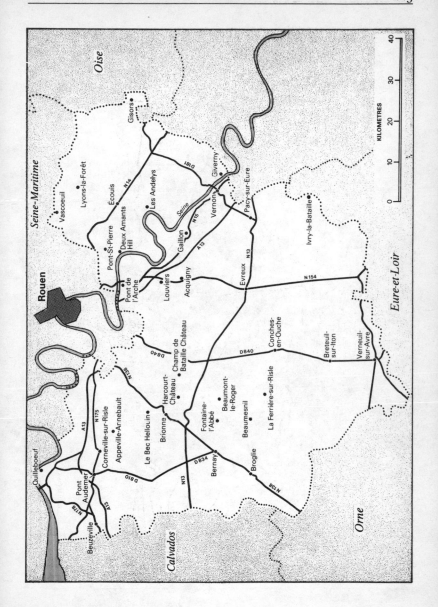

4 *Eure*

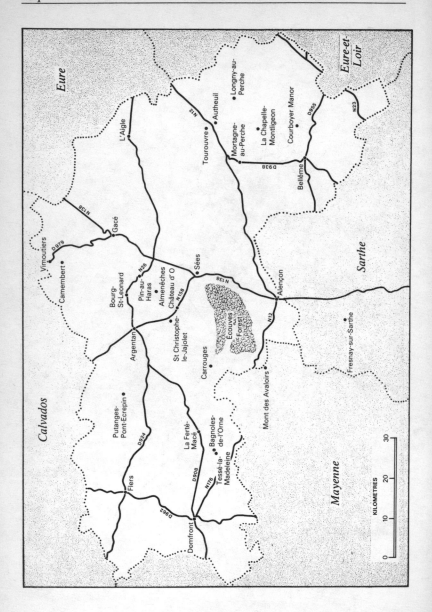

5 *Orne*

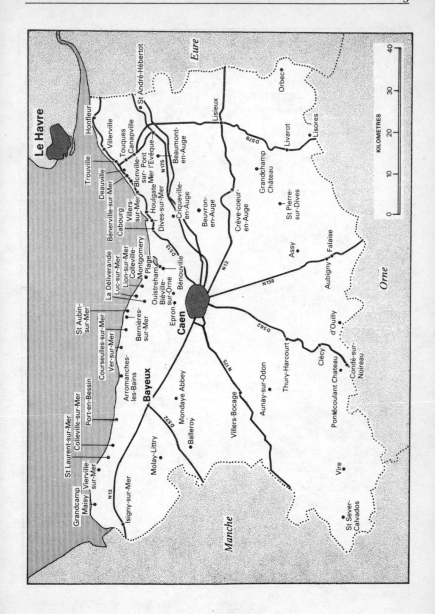

6 *Calvados*

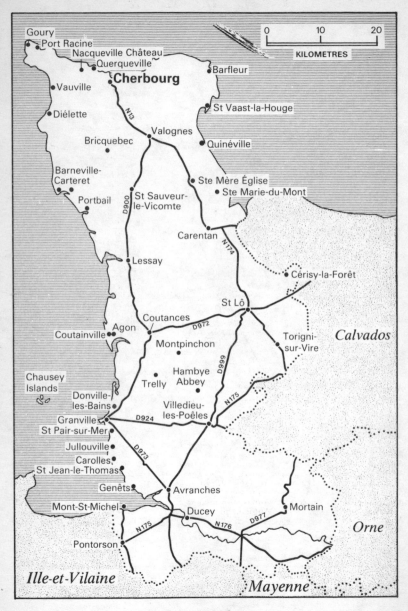

7 *Manche*

INDEX

Index compiled by Peva Keane